T0383640

Practical Cloud Security
A Cross-Industry View

Practical Cloud Security
A Cross-Industry View

Melvin B. Greer, Jr.
National Cybersecurity Institute,
Washington, District of Columbia, USA

Kevin L. Jackson
CloudGov Network, LLC,
Washington, District of Columbia, USA

CRC Press
Taylor & Francis Group
Boca Raton London New York

CRC Press is an imprint of the
Taylor & Francis Group, an **informa** business

CRC Press
Taylor & Francis Group
6000 Broken Sound Parkway NW, Suite 300
Boca Raton, FL 33487-2742

© 2017 by Taylor & Francis Group, LLC
CRC Press is an imprint of Taylor & Francis Group, an Informa business

No claim to original U.S. Government works

Printed on acid-free paper
Version Date: 20160325

International Standard Book Number-13: 978-1-4987-2943-7 (Hardback)

Library of Congress Cataloging-in-Publication Data

Names: Greer, Melvin B., Jr., author. | Jackson, Kevin L., author.
Title: Practical cloud security : a cross-industry view / Melvin B. Greer, Jr., and Kevin L. Jackson.
Description: Boca Raton : CRC Press, 2016.
Identifiers: LCCN 2016003428 | ISBN 9781498729437 (hardcover : acid-free paper)
Subjects: LCSH: Cloud computing--Security measures. | Cloud computing--Industrial applications.
Classification: LCC QA76.585 .G84 2016 | DDC 004.67/82--dc23
LC record available at http://lccn.loc.gov/2016003428

Visit the Taylor & Francis Web site at
http://www.taylorandfrancis.com

and the CRC Press Web site at
http://www.crcpress.com

Printed and bound in the United States of America by Publishers Graphics, LLC on sustainably sourced paper.

Contents

Foreword

THERE IS, BY NOW, no doubt that we are living in the digital era. Globally renowned thought-leader Don Tapscott refers to it as the "Age of Networked Intelligence." Leading venture capitalist Marc Andreessen claims that "Software Is Eating the World." Yet another leading VC, Mary Meeker, describes how industry after industry is being "reimagined." This reimagination means that enormous wealth is being created by companies that are in some cases barely out of their teens, or not even that old: Google, Amazon, Facebook, Snapchat, Tesla, and Uber. Other companies and industries are being reimagined into oblivion, or at least forced reinvention: Blockbuster, Borders Books, *Encyclopedia Britannica*'s print edition, newspapers, CDs, taxis, DVDs, landline telephony, cable TV services.

The enablers of this transformation include voracious consumers; an entrepreneurial culture; unprecedented access to capital thanks to low or nonexistent interest rates, venture capital, and angel investors who cashed out in the last wave of market expansion; and a rise in global flows of goods, services, capital, and information; together with global prosperity as measured by metrics such as standard of living. Another key enabler, which some might argue is the most key, is a constellation of technologies: the Internet; mobile and wireline broadband networking; big data and analytics; and smart, digital, connected things ranging from jet engines to smart pills to autonomous vehicles.

At the nexus of all of these technologies and trends lies Cloud Computing. Simply put, Cloud Computing enables consumers, small businesses, corporations, and governments to easily access computing resources with little or no upfront investment or commitment. It thus mirrors the ease of accessing a hotel room, compared with the perseverance and pain of saving for years or decades to buy a home. Stated in this way, the value of Cloud Computing would appear to be simple—say, a straightforward financial equation—but it's not.

In my most recent book, *Digital Disciplines*, I delineate four generic strategies that companies can use to exploit the power of software, the cloud, and related digital technologies. One approach is to complement physical operational excellence in processes and resource use with information excellence by, for example, optimizing physical operations with advanced algorithms or seamlessly fusing the online and offline worlds. The second is to move beyond product or service leadership to leadership in smart, digital, connected products and services, thus enabling extensibility, new business models, and a focus on customer experiences and outcomes. A third is to transcend or complement face-to-face human-mediated relationships with virtual, algorithmically mediated ones through collective intimacy by leveraging social networks but also recommendation engines and other predictive analytics. The fourth, overarching strategy is to accelerate innovation through cloud-centric approaches such as idea markets, innovation networks, crowdsourcing, and online contests and challenges.

Practically any entrepreneur with an idea and an Internet connection can execute these strategies and rapidly prototype anything and everything required to run a virtual business. Today's technologies and on-demand information services mean that capitalism no longer requires capital, or people, for that matter. In the industrial age, infrastructure for service delivery such as railroads or manufacturing operations such as factories required massive amounts of capital for things such as locomotives, basic oxygen furnaces, and assembly lines. Today, all you need is a little luck, an idea, a laptop, and a credit card for the means of production, and an app store or the web for the means of distribution.

Companies can produce a billion dollars in annual revenue with a handful of employees. This, in turn, means that larger, more established companies must pay attention to these trends and enablers, whether they want to or not. Weight Watchers has tens of thousands of employees, but competes with MyFitnessPal, a diet/nutrition/exercise app company with 50 employees. It was acquired by Under Armour for almost half a billion (US) dollars after just 10 years of operation. Global telcos have hundreds of millions of employees, but their highly profitable SMS and related messaging services compete with WhatsApp, another company with about 50 employees and almost a billion users. WhatsApp was acquired by Facebook for US$19 billion barely 5 years after its founding. The lesson is clear: A company can't just cast a watchful eye at long-time competitors in its industry, but must be wary of competitors from other industries and upstart start-ups.

Unfortunately, the converse of the maxim that every cloud has a silver lining is that every sun also has sunspots—dark regions in the sea of light. The same attributes that make the Internet, the cloud, and software so powerful also make them dangerous. The global access that enables anyone to download a book to their mobile device also allows anyone from a bored teen looking for a thrill to a criminal cybergang looking for a payday to a government bent on projecting influence to wreak havoc with corporations or nations. And, they can attack an enterprise a world away from the comfort of their own living room or the Starbucks around the corner.

In many ways, the cloud offers greater security than most firms can offer in their own data centers; whether physical facility security, protection from network-based attacks, or hiring and maintaining the best and the brightest to audit, ethically hack, and improve practices and products. And anyone who argues that the cloud is not 100% secure is technically accurate, but then nothing can ever be 100% secure. That said, the cloud introduces new vulnerabilities, because it is a shared environment, which is globally accessible.

Moreover, the cloud, of course, runs software applications. Software is powerful because of the infinite combinations in which lines of code can create new functional constructs, new artifacts, and new business models. But the power of software is also its weakness, because these infinite combinations lead to infinite complexity, and therefore lead to the inability of any individual to truly understand how the software actually works under all conditions, including deliberate attack. Consider the case of Heartbleed, considered a "catastrophic" bug, which exposed a substantial fraction of the world's websites to unauthorized data access. It reportedly was due to a trivial programming error introduced by a well-meaning software developer contributing his time to an open source project.

Executives and boards have always had to manage risk. Now, the executive risk management portfolio must include cybersecurity. To ignore it is fraught with broad potential for disaster. As cyberspace has become the new frontier of the economy, or perhaps even civilization, as we know it, it has also become a battleground. This means that executives can no longer ignore security, washing their hands of it and relegating it to "the security guy," whether male or female. This isn't hyperbole, but a matter of record.

Consider the Target data breach of 2013, which impacted tens of millions of customers at Target, one of the world's largest retailers. It led to a dramatic drop in Target's revenues and profits as disgruntled customers defected and Target not only lost business but had to spend money on recovery and mitigation and agree to financial settlements with card issuers such as Visa. It also led to massive impacts upon *customers* as they had credit and debit cards cancelled due to the breach and were unable to shop *anywhere.*

Any executive will understand the additional personal—and personnel—repercussions: Not only were Target shareholders, partners, and customers affected, so was the executive team. CIO Beth Jacob was replaced, as might be expected. But in addition, underscoring how the "C" in "C suite" now also encompasses cybersecurity, CEO Gregg Steinhafel, a 35-year veteran of the company, resigned following the breach.

It isn't just companies, but governments and their various branches, agencies, or bureaus as well. A breach at the US Office of Personnel Management led to unauthorized access of perhaps close to 20 million records. As with Target, the buck stopped with the top executive, Katherine Archuleta, who resigned shortly after details of the breach became public.

This is not to pick on Target or OPM: it seems virtually every company has a breach sooner or later, across verticals: Home Depot, Heartland Payment Systems, Neiman Marcus, T.J. Maxx, JPMorgan Chase, Sony Online Entertainment, Anthem, the list goes on and on. It's also not to pick on Archuleta, Jacob, or Steinhafel; they very well may have been doing not only the best job that they could do, but the best that anyone could have done.

The important lesson for executives, within and outside of the IT function, is that as the economy becomes increasingly digital, the job of today's corporate or government leader now encompasses not just financial results, customer and employee satisfaction, strategic vision and execution, and communications skills but also understanding not only competitive threats but information security ones as well.

This new category of threat is *based* on information but is not *restricted* to information. As the virtual and physical worlds become increasingly connected, cyberattacks can do more than steal credit card and social security numbers or hold digital wedding and graduation photos for ransom; they can create catastrophic impacts through cyber-physical systems and connections. The Stuxnet attack on Iranian centrifuges was as effective as physical bombardment might have been. A German steel mill was recently destroyed via a remote cyberattack. Every nation's critical infrastructure—banks, aviation, power plants, dams, factories, and railroads—is potentially vulnerable. As armies increasingly become made up of robot soldiers, drones, and connected weapons systems, a single errant line of code, virus, Trojan, or buffer overflow may do more to turn the tide of war than an entire division or army.

And information security is only one dimension of the multifaceted problem of maximizing the return from information technology while minimizing downside. After all, today's customers, whether consumers or businesses, employees, partners, or citizens, have high expectations around the total experience, including ease of use, navigability, availability, privacy, security, and aesthetics. Global hypercompetition leads to compressed time frames, which can force companies to focus on minimum viable products and thus speed products to market, but can also cause software quality and vulnerability issues. And, finding qualified staff to address all these facets is a challenge that seems to be getting worse, not better.

Melvin B. Greer, Jr. and Kevin L. Jackson have assembled a comprehensive guide to cybersecurity, which can serve multiple purposes, not the least of which is documenting the breadth and severity of the challenges that today's enterprises face, and the breadth of programmatic elements required to address these challenges. This has become a boardroom issue: executives must not only exploit the potential of information technologies but also manage their potential risks.

As the saying goes in regard to the law, ignorance is no excuse. With Jackson and Greer's book, there is now no excuse for ignorance.

Joe Weinman
Author, Cloudonomics: The Business Value of Cloud Computing and Digital Disciplines: Attaining Market Leadership via the Cloud, Big Data, Social, Mobile, and the Internet of Things

A link to the authors' website for extended multimedia content is available from the CRC Press website: http://www.crcpress.com/product/isbn /9781498729437.

Extended Multimedia Content

Thank you for purchasing *Practical Cloud Security:*
A Cross-Industry View

WHILE THE PHYSICAL TEXT is a critical component of any learning environment, the authors also believe in the enhancement value of multimedia content. In support of that viewpoint, they have also produced a set of companion videos that can be used to augment any related training or education curriculum. This multimedia content is available online at www.oncloudtraining.com for a nominal additional fee.

Book Topic	Page	Extended Multimedia Content
Chapter 2 Economics of Cloud Computing	11	**Business Innovation** • Cloud Computing Business Models • Cloud Adoption Strategies • Business KPIs and Goals • Cloud Adoption Life Cycle • Cloud Computing Return on Investment • Business Value of Information Technology • The Economic Benefit of Cloud Computing • Cloud Computing Business Context • Cloud Business Case Development
Chapter 5 Cloud Computing	46	**Cloud Basics** • What Is Cloud Computing? • Traditional Computing Challenges and Concerns • Cloud Computing Benefits • Cloud Computing Challenges and Inhibitors • Cloud Use Cases and Examples • Cloud Computing Frameworks

Introduction

WHILE CLOUD COMPUTING IS a technical evolution, its effects on industry markets have been revolutionary. The blend of highly automated information technology with various industry business models has created an explosion of technology-driven business service solutions. These hybrid creations not only birth new marketplaces but also spawn industry-specific cloud security challenges.

While these challenges have understandably driven a heightened security concern, there has been a lack of industry-specific cloud security information and education. The single exception to this general rule has been within the government industry where the US federal government's "Cloud First" strategy led to the development of the Federal Risk Authorization and Risk Management Program. This book is a start toward remedying this current reality.

In order to gain insight from industry practitioners, primary research data on the views of enterprise chief information security officers (CISOs) are also included in this text. Conducted in collaboration with the National Cybersecurity Institute and Dell Corporation, these data were collected through an online survey in the spring of 2015. The CISO Survey specifically mentioned 10 industries:

- Energy/Utilities

- Telecommunications

- Banking/Finance

- Transportation

- Healthcare

- Information Technology

- Food and Agriculture

- Education

- Manufacturing

- Security Consulting Service

Although responses from telecommunications, transportation, food and agriculture, and manufacturing industries were also sought, the responses were insufficient for analysis. The level of response from government industry vertical warranted the addition of that group into the primary data analysis.

Industry approach to cybersecurity analyses is compared across the following domains:

- Organizational Reporting

- Training and Education

- Demographics

- Operational Planning

- Operations

- Cloud Computing

The analysis process documented a broad marketplace snapshot based on data. The study team compared each industry vertical snapshot to the marketplace and evaluated them with respect to marketplace consistency. In some cases, follow-up interviews with industry representatives were also conducted. The interviews were used to

- Validate trends and any major deviations

- Identify industry-relevant or -specific best practices for marketplace trends

- Identify industry-relevant or -specific best practices for deviations

- Compare industry-relevant or -specific best practices to industry general best practices

- Develop conclusions and recommendations

Study results are included when applicable.

After giving a general overview of both Cloud Computing and cyber-security, this text will then look at the role of the CISO. As the key executive responsible for cloud security, the general views of these practitioners will help frame the industry-specific analysis and recommendations that follow.

CHAPTER 1

Cloud User Perceptions

IN 2015, CLOUD SERVICE users were asked about their perceptions regarding personal data security.* The results were tabulated and ranked by industry. Levels of concern about cybersecurity are high in some US industry sectors. Depending on the type of organization, the expectation that a security breach is likely within the next 12 months ranges from 21% for utilities to nearly half (44%) for retailers.

Consumers were most concerned about compromise of their personal data with retail, attributed to recent high profile data breaches. There was significant concern about government organizations as well, a result of the recently reported cyberattacks. The low perceived risk of a data breach with banks is possibly a reflection of the traditionally high levels of trust in the security of these organizations and government organizations.

---

* http://assets.unisys.com/Documents/Microsites/UnisysSecurityInsights/USI_150227_USreport
.pdf.

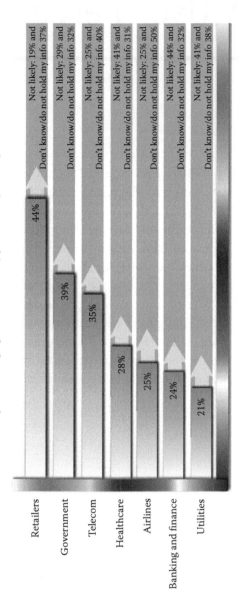

Comparison of high-profile vulnerability prevalence by industry vertical

Retailers — 44% — Not likely: 19% and Don't know/do not hold my info 37%

Government — 39% — Not likely: 29% and Don't know/do not hold my info 32%

Telecom — 35% — Not likely: 25% and Don't know/do not hold my info 40%

Healthcare — 28% — Not likely: 41% and Don't know/do not hold my info 31%

Airlines — 25% — Not likely: 25% and Don't know/do not hold my info 50%

Banking and finance — 24% — Not likely: 44% and Don't know/do not hold my info 32%

Utilities — 21% — Not likely: 41% and Don't know/do not hold my info 38%

CHAPTER 2

Economics of Cloud Computing

WHILE SECURITY HAS BEEN and will continue to be a key enterprise concern, the widespread focus on this single aspect has overshadowed the critically important economic and operational underpinnings of this new model. This unfortunate reality has skewed Cloud Computing training and education away from the business aspects, which are crucial to any successful enterprise transition. In his book, *Cloudonomics: The Business Value of Cloud Computing*, Joe Weinman (2012) provided a very concise treatment of these operational and economic aspects. The authors have relied heavily on this text as a reference for the following section as a thorough understanding of business linkages is fundamental to the development of practical and operationally acceptable security strategies and policies.

Over the past few years, information technology (IT) investments by companies have been definitively linked with productivity increases. These productivity increases, however, have not necessarily led to improved profitability or market share. This is primarily attributed to companies using these productivity increases to reduce cost for end consumers. It has also led to the growth of a camp that classifies cloud as merely a technological evolution.

An opposing camp takes to heart data that point specifically to Cloud Computing investments, not general IT investments, as the reason for recent rapid productivity growth. While this point of view is overhyped by many, the ubiquitous reach and democratizing effect on the consumption of commodity IT services demonstrably create value. This has made cloud a tactical necessity in many industries. It has also become a strategic differentiator in others. While one should never ignore traditional business principles and metrics, such as revenues and profits, digital businesses that have been "born-in-the-cloud" have challenged many traditional business assumptions (Exhibit 2.1). Such contradictory realities make it very confusing for today's chief information officer (CIO) when tasked to develop an enterprise Cloud Computing strategy. In fact the entire C-suite is forced to deal with, "… new models, where partnerships are dynamic and based on platforms; services aren't 'delivered' but co-created with customers and partners; these services don't have value until the customer applies them in context; and the way to make money can be by giving things away, as hardware vendors do with open source software" (Weinman 2012, p. 30).

When developing any type of strategy, the CIO must have the creation of a sustainable marketplace advantage as their primary goal. Part and parcel to that strategic goal is delivering value to the organization's external and internal customers. Value is a very complex metric because, from a strategic point of view, it is a function of customer wants and needs, capabilities and competencies relative to the competition, and the global

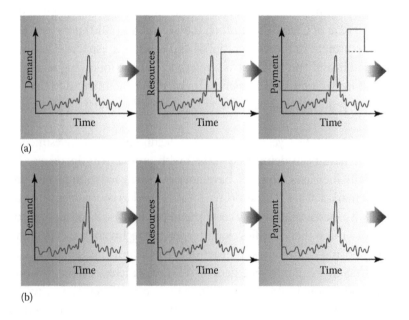

EXHIBIT 2.1   Traditional versus cloud model. (a) Traditional model and (b) on demand, pay per use.

environment. The environment itself is equally complex because it consists of macroeconomic factors, regional growth, regulatory and legal constraints, and others. Although the time frame has been relative short, the industry has already discovered some cloud-compatible and cloud-incompatible high-level strategies.

Compatible strategies include the following:

- Complementary Capabilities and Competencies—when cloud provides a competency that your organization doesn't possess

- Communications—when a communication option such as voice, video chat, texting, direct messaging, or e-mail is enabled or optimized through the use of a cloud-based architecture

- Conversations, Connections, and Communities—the use of global networks to help forge strong bonds and useful weak ties between geographically dispersed individuals

- Congregations, Commons, and Collections—building, moderating, or managing collections of people or things

- Consolidation—enabling the de-duplication of data, information, or resources

- Collaboration, Competition, and Crowdsourcing—enabling shared repositories of work as well as synchronous and asynchronous communications and creating and maintaining a permanent archive of ephemeral digital communications

- Commerce and Clearing—creation of marketplaces that bring buyers and sellers together within a common framework that avoids unmanageable numbers of pairwise connections

- Collaborative Consumption—creation of "communal economies" and "redistribution markets" by connecting people with goods to the people who want those goods

- Coordination, Currency, Consistency, and Control—an efficient enabler of communication that can coordinate events or ensure status consistency

- Cross-Device Access and Synchronization—synchronization of content or applications across a single user with multiple devices

- Cash Flow—changing capital expenditures into operational expenditures
- Capacity—complementing existing, owned data center capacity with cloud capacity
- Continuity—avoid procuring and operating duplicative business continuity hardware by storing business continuity–related data and applications in the cloud
- Checkpoints—serve as an enterprise IT infrastructure entry checkpoint to filter threats such as viruses, spam, and distributed denial of service attacks
- Chokepoints—throttling, policing, shaping, limiting, and managing data traffic in accordance with enterprise policy in order to ensure better overall service
- Context—pursuit of an enterprise strategy that retains core activities within the enterprise and moving context activities, such as expense reporting, funnel management, and billing, to the cloud
- Celerity—increasing business operational speed through the use of Software as a Service (SaaS), Platform as a Service (PaaS), or Infrastructure as a Service (IaaS)
- Customer Experience—enhance customer experience through geographical dispersion of content and applications

Incompatible high-level strategies include the following:

- Constant—flat and predictable IT demands
- Custom—specific and highly customized architectures
- Classic—substantial legacy software code base
- Close Coupling—use of applications that are tightly coupled to predictable, custom, and legacy applications because of either high bandwidth or extreme latency constraints for interprocess communication or data transport to and from storage systems or other devices
- Content Capture, Creation, and Consumption—use with content that is originally captured at the edge via end user devices and delivered, displayed, and consumed at the same edge

- Cryptography—encryption of content captured at an edge user device
- Compression—compression of content captured at an edge user device
- Caching—caching of content captured at an edge user device
- Covert—data or information that would put the organization in legal or regulatory extremis
- Continuity—activities that are required in the event of connectivity loss, cloud service outage, provider financial instability, or when untethered

The compatibility of certain strategies with Cloud Computing is not based on anecdotes but on quantitative modeling and research. Some of the most important ones are as follows:

- Smart Network Optimization—The theory that networks should be "stupid" and provide "dumb pipes," that is, all intelligence should be at the endpoints. Simulations show that route optimization based on consideration of both server response time and path latency can lead to optimized performance. The degree of improvement is coupled to the number of optional path and server combinations: the more options, the greater the speedup, but with diminishing returns to scale. The simulation model supports theoretical analysis based on expected values of minimum values given the order statistics calculated using beta distribution.*

- Hub-and-Spoke versus Point-to-Point—This analysis addresses trade-offs in the design of networks, whether they be highways, airport location and flight routing, or communications networks. One strategy is the point-to-point network, which offers the shortest possible distance and therefore latency between any two points, but at the expense of a quadratically increasing number of connections. Another option is the hub-and-spoke network, which requires fewer total links growing linearly in the number of nodes, but can increase latency, as any traveler who has had to change planes and fly indirect routes knows. This model provides Monte Carlo simulation support for the theoretical expected values.†

---

* http://www.complexmodels.com/NetworkOptionsHelp.htm.
† http://www.complexmodels.com/HubOrDirectHelp.aspx.

- The Market for Melons: Quantity Uncertainty and the Market Mechanism—This model is based on Joe Weinman's "The Market for Melons" analysis and simulates a duopoly with one flat-rate, one pay-per-use provider, and customers with dispersed heterogeneous consumption. The flat-rate price always reflects the average consumption of the patrons of the flat-rate provider, whereas the pay-per-use provider price is based on each customer's exact usage. Initially, heavy users migrate to the flat-rate plan and light users migrate to the pay-per-use one. This causes price rises with more repercussions, until eventually virtually all customers are patrons of pay-per-use.[*]

- Value of Utility Resources in the Cloud—This model illustrates the relationship between various demand curves, capacity strategies addressing those types of demand singly or in combination, and the economics of trade-offs. Is it better to use solely static capacity engineered to peak demand? Or to use less static capacity and accept penalties associated with inability to meet peak requirements (e.g., loss of revenue associated with unserved customers)? Or use purely utility resources to meet all demand? Or to use a hybrid approach? The answer is: it depends, and this model shows the relationships between the different factors that would lead to an optimal selection.[†]

- Value of Resource Pooling and Load Sharing across a Grid—This model illustrates the benefits of pooling resources, which may be geographically dispersed. Aligning each demand source individually with a partitioned set of resources means that each set of resources must be engineered to meet the peak demand associated with that resource. Pooling resources and meeting demand via any available resource has the benefit that the capacity required is not the sum of the peak demand, but the peak of the sum of the demands, which is probably no larger, and is typically smaller. Consequently, pooling resources and distributing load across them is usually a good idea (subject to ancillary costs not addressed in this model). A special case of this is geographic dispersion across time zones, where some demand types, for example, 9-to-5 weekday work, can lead to dramatic savings through a "follow the sun" approach.[‡]

---

[*] http://www.joeweinman.com/Resources/Joe_Weinman_The_Market_For_%20Melons.pdf.
[†] http://www.complexmodels.com/UtilityHelp.aspx.
[‡] http://www.complexmodels.com/GridHelp.aspx.

- Value of Dispersion in Latency Reduction—This model illustrates the benefits of dispersion for latency reduction, as well as the diminishing returns of additional node builds, leading to a "sweet spot" number of nodes. This model is relevant in scenarios as diverse as locating coffee shops, fast-food restaurants, distributed interactive computing environments, and content delivery architectures. Dispersion can have additional benefits, for example, enhanced business continuity, as well as costs, for example, operations and real estate, but these are not modeled here.*

- Value of Aggregation in Variability Smoothing and Peak Reduction—This model illustrates the two main benefits of aggregating demand: reduction in peak capacity requirements and increase in utilization. The increase in utilization comes about in two ways. One is that the same demand is served by a smaller-sized pro forma capacity, but the second is that aggregation of random variables preserves absolute variance but reduces relative variance. The so-called coefficient of variation is a measure of variability relative to the mean, and this is reduced as more and more random variables are summed. In a cloud or utility environment, this is one of the drivers of service provider economics.†

- Central Limit Theorem and Combinatorics—This model also illustrates the benefits of aggregating demand: reduction in peak capacity requirements as well as increase in utilization. Strictly speaking, the peak does not change across all possible combinations, but the mass near the peak does, therefore reducing the cost of unserved demand. The distribution of the sum increasingly is normal, in accordance with the Central Limit Theorem. This model shows the effect by determining the distribution of sums of dice that are randomly rolled and seeing how summing more and more dice results in a tighter (reduced coefficient of variation) distribution.‡

- Network Evolution via Preferential Attachment—Mathematical modeling and empirical analysis of Internet connectivity by professor and author Albert-Laszlo Barabasi has demonstrated that network evolution by "preferential attachment" leads to so-called

---

* http://www.complexmodels.com/LatencyHelp.aspx.
† http://www.complexmodels.com/AggregationHelp.aspx.
‡ http://www.complexmodels.com/CentralLimitHelp.aspx.

power-law, aristocratic, or scale-free node degree distributions. In other words, the "rich" nodes get "richer" as new entrants to the network preferentially decide to attach to them. This simulation shows the difference between preferential attachment and random attachment, up to just more than 1000 nodes, and enables viewing of the resulting network from both a node degree distribution perspective and an actual graph.*

- Yard-Sale Simulation: The Rich Get Richer—In *Group Theory in the Bedroom*, Brian Hayes reviews so-called Yard-Sale Simulations, or asset exchange models, where pairwise traders operate in a market on a zero-sum basis to randomly win or lose trades. For very small "bets" and short periods, an initially equal distribution of wealth will evolve to a normal distribution, as wins and losses tend to cancel each other out. However, for larger bets or longer periods, the market evolves to concentrate wealth increasingly, eventually resulting in a "winner-take-all" result. This is because once a trader goes broke, no matter how unlikely that is, they cannot reenter the market. Interestingly, even when wealth is initially equal across all traders, it can rapidly evolve to a power-law or exponential distribution.†

- Investor Risk—This is a simplified version of the Yard-Sale simulation. Investors either win or lose on each trial, with the amount of the gain or loss dependent on the investment rules. Because of Brownian effects, eventually investors can go broke, at which point they exit the system. This results in increasing concentration of wealth. Different rules lead to different distributions: an equal distribution of wealth evolves to a normal distribution and shifts to what appears to be a power-law or exponential distribution.‡

- Random Walks—This illustrates the random processes at work behind such phenomena as Brownian motion. Ten particles begin the simulation in the same location, but then move, each trial, based on a rule. Some variations are one-dimensional, while others are two-dimensional. The one-dimensional rule is similar to a simplified version of the investor risk model, which is a simplified version

* http://www.complexmodels.com/AristoHelp.aspx.
† http://www.complexmodels.com/TradingHelp.aspx.
‡ http://www.complexmodels.com/InvestorHelp.aspx.

of the asset exchange model (yard-sale simulation). The only difference is that any particle (i.e., investor) can go deeply into debt and
so remains in the simulation. Consequently, rags to riches is not
unlikely.*

Cloud is also a cross-domain concept, not restricted to computing and
IT. Offline analogies abound, including "a big data repository in the cloud
is analogous to the New York Public Library or the Library of Congress;
collaboration via the cloud is not much different than gathering in a conference room; markets where buyers and sellers can meet on line are not
much different than flea markets or the trading floor of the New York
Stock Exchange."

In developing a cloud strategy, the CIO must deal with the disparity
between the capacity to produce products and deliver services—which
is fixed in the short term—and the demand for those products and
services—which is almost always variable at any time scale. Customer
demand in just about any circumstance is volatile. While some tactical
measures can be taken to alleviate some scenarios, Cloud Computing
models have been shown to be capable of solving the so-called Demand
Dilemma when they are applied to Cloud Computing compatible business models.

A similar issue, sometimes referred to as the "Capacity Conundrum,"
can similarly be effectively addressed with Cloud Computing. Exemplary
of this business challenge is when a company builds capacity to match
peak demand. It will realize substantial excess capacity during off-peak
periods. This excess capacity represents either nonproductive capital or
unnecessary expense. Conversely, if capacity is sized to the baseline, there
will be insufficient resources to handle spikes. Transactions not served
represent demand for the products or services that the business would
have monetized, resulting in lost revenue or lost worker productivity.

Cloud Computing strategies should also look toward leveraging scale.
While this Cloud Computing advantage may certainly be capable of delivering resources and services at a lower unit cost than an enterprise, even
if the cloud is more expensive on a unit-cost basis, it can still cost less,
in terms of total cost of ownership. While making an exact comparison
between internal costs and external prices is complex, such costs may be as
much a matter of culture and practices as they are on financial transaction

---

* http://www.complexmodels.com/BrownianHelp.aspx.

data. The logic of this analysis means that Cloud Computing should be a component of every organization's IT strategy regardless of the individual transaction costs.

The logic also highlights the concept of hybrid clouds where the presence of variable demand and a utility premium for cloud resources can lead to a more optimal operational mix. There are several different permutations of hybrids including dedicated flat-rate resources and on-demand pay-per-use resources (Exhibit 2.2).

Generic hybrid cloud options include the following (Exhibit 2.3):

- User to enterprise resources—user connects only to enterprise

- User to cloud resources—user connects only to cloud resources

Specific hybrid cloud options include the following:

- Colocated Hybrid

- Partitioned-Data Hybrid

- Monolithic Hybrid with Remote Data Access

- Monolithic Hybrid with Dynamic Data Migration

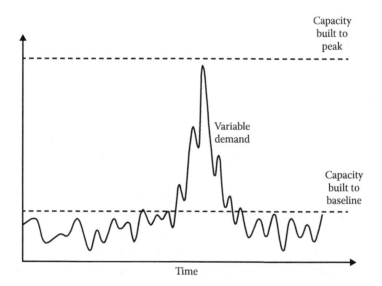

EXHIBIT 2.2   Fixed capacity is a poor solution to variable demand.

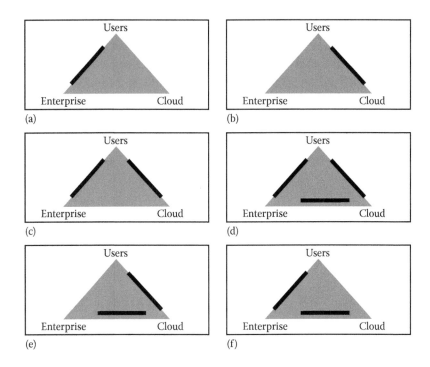

EXHIBIT 2.3   Generic architecture options.

- Monolithic Hybrid with Data Synchronization
- Eventual Consistency
- Front-End/Back-End Hybrids
- On-Demand BC/DR

Using hybrid cloud options also provides source diversification with respect to IT services. For much the reason that financial advisors recommend stock portfolio diversification, hybrid solutions leverage a mathematical characteristic of the sum of independent random variables. Cloud service providers can use this statistical effect to generate a compelling economic value proposition. In this way, strategic use of hybrid cloud solutions can also significantly reduce enterprise costs related to inaccurate IT requirement and capacity forecasts.

The dynamic responsiveness and the parallel nature of cloud are also used to replace operational restriction of serial processes on limited infrastructure with parallel business processes hosted on highly dynamic on-demand infrastructures. "Google uses this strategy every time someone runs a search. Rather than poking along on a single processor, Google uses 1000 or more, thereby returning results in milliseconds, in turn increasing click-throughs, thereby ringing the cash registers in Mountain View to the tune of $40 billion each year" (Weinman 2012, p. 236).

Parallelism can also be used to reduce application response time. There are, however, diminishing returns after early gains if enterprises are using the traditional, organic infrastructure model. In these situations, the cloud can be a huge benefit by providing an alternative to long delays caused by limited resources, and delivering many resources in parallel at essentially no additional cost (Exhibits 2.4 and 2.5).

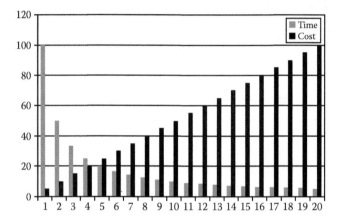

EXHIBIT 2.4   Without cloud: diminishing returns from parallelization with linear costs.

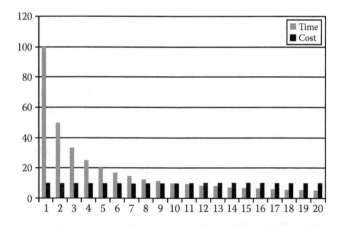

EXHIBIT 2.5   Without cloud: constant costs regardless of parallelization.

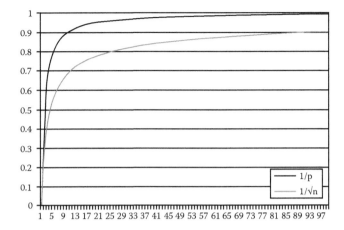

EXHIBIT 2.6   Relative response time reduction from increased parallelism versus increased dispersion.

For companies looking to reduce response time via dispersion of resources, a roughly similar analysis holds. Increasing the number of delivery points can reduce time attributed to network latency by reducing the average or worst-case distance between a user and a service node. Using organic funds to pursue this form of operational improvement can become prohibitively expensive also because of diminishing returns. Once again, the cloud can help by providing pay-per-use access to resources.

Consolidation generally has benefits, such as aggregate demand smoothing, ability to leverage parallelism, and economies of scale. Dispersion has benefits in the way of a further reduction in response time for interactive applications. An organization's decision on which strategy to use depends on the industry, customer set, business model, and corporate goals (Exhibit 2.6).

REFERENCE

Weinman, J. 2012. *Cloudonomics: The Business Value of Cloud Computing.* John Wiley & Sons.

CHAPTER 3

Process and Sources

CHIEF INFORMATION SECURITY OFFICERS (CISOs) from 30 industries had been invited to participate in the March 2015 research survey. More than 500 CISOs in the United States were sent electronic invitations and more than 100 participated. GovCloud Network LLC and Dell Inc. solicited respondents primarily through Twitter, LinkedIn, and e-mail and the International Information Systems Security Certification Consortium. This unique survey looks to understand the evolving CISO role. As a result of the survey, we are able to expand our understanding of next-generation CISOs and their organization. The respondents provided information about the education and professional background of CISOs. We understand the impact of experiences on career path. Demographics give us a contextual view and a way to compare CISOs within a group and between groups. The CISO Survey examines the CISO role in a number of key industry verticals including healthcare, telecommunications, utilities/energy, finance, transportation, government, and agriculture. The survey goals are to determine the factors that drive the CISO profile, including the following:

- Demographics
- Experience
- CISO requirements
- CISO effectiveness and alignment
- CISO focus and priorities

Through an interactive process with the National Cybersecurity Institute, the survey was designed and developed using Qualtrics so as to explicitly address National Cybersecurity Institute tactical and strategic research goals. These goals include but were not limited to the following:

- Industry
- Respondent Seniority
- Automated Platform Usage
- Geographic Location
- Cybersecurity Professional Certification

After creation of a baseline target list of interview questions, the questions were augmented with relevant National Cybersecurity Institute–provided data. The raw survey data collected have been categorized with respect to industry, geographic location, and respondent cybersecurity professional certification.

Analysis of the data focused on identification of important cybersecurity-related issues and trends from both industry-specific and cross-industry perspectives. The analysis activities paid particular attention to data related to the National Cybersecurity Institute's tactical and strategic interests in critical infrastructures.

The goal of this report is to provide a better understanding of the CISO role in the critical infrastructure industries as well as to identify specific CISO practices and behaviors that could strengthen the role and influence of other CISOs.

Melvin Greer and Kevin L. Jackson, National Cybersecurity Institute at Excelsior College Fellows, have conducted this CISO Industry Survey and corresponding report. The CISO Survey findings clarify the CISO role in a number of key industry verticals including healthcare, telecommunications, utilities/energy, finance, transportation, government, and agriculture. This survey report has been used to illuminate issues on education of CISOs, demographics, and organizational reporting. The CISO role is evolving and this survey reinforces the idea that all industries are not only aggressively hiring CISOs but also including them in strategic decision making.

CHAPTER 4

Industry-Specific Findings

4.1 OFFICIAL TITLES

Having an official title of chief information security officer (CISO) seems less likely as director, manager, and chief compliance officer. The data also suggest that the responsibilities associated with providing enterprise-wide security are spread across a number of different but related job titles depending on the organization. Given the importance of cybersecurity to the workings of the enterprise and the potential negative impact of data breaches and security threats, it is no wonder that high-level CISOs report to the chief executive officer (CEO)/president. Additionally, government CISOs report to Federal agency senior leadership or the compliance officer. Reporting to the chief information officer (CIO) or chief financial officer (CFO) would rank second overall.

Professionals that hold this key position had varied backgrounds. CISOs have great responsibility, and 75% note that they also have authority to enforce compliance. On the basis of the data, however, most in government do not. CISOs report the need for multidisciplinary skills in carrying out their duties. Common are information technology (IT) and communication. More than 77% report that business knowledge is critical to the success of their role.

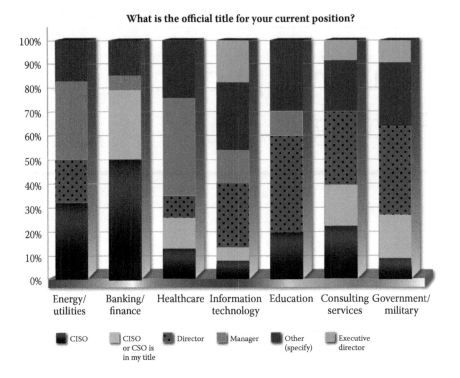

What is the official title for your current position?

4.2 HIGHEST LEVEL OF EDUCATION

The report indicates a key trend in the education requirements for CISOs. More than 76% report that they have attained a bachelor degree or higher, and almost 85% report that Information Systems Security certification is a baseline requirement for the role.

Operationally, CISOs are generally satisfied with the quality of their network's IT/Cybersecurity controls but they also see cyberattacks as a major threat. Targeted attacks and malware are of major concern, with activist and criminal groups as the most likely source.

Years in industry

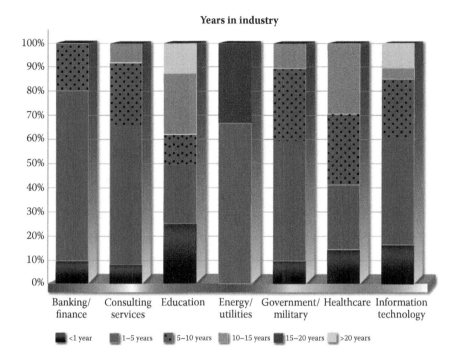

■ <1 year ■ 1–5 years ■ 5–10 years ■ 10–15 years ■ 15–20 years □ >20 years

4.3 INDUSTRY REPRESENTATION

While government is not ranked in the top three—IT (23%), banking/finance (14%), and consulting services (13%)—the vast majority of "other" (19%) includes government, federal government, Fed Gov't/DoD, defense, military, public service, and intelligence.

4.4 ORGANIZATIONAL REPORTING

According to the study, CISOs believe that their functional responsibility should report to a senior executive in the organization. Almost 80% report that they believe CISOs should report to the CEO, CIO, or an executive VP. Many include reporting directly to the board of directors or reporting to but with actionable independence from the CEO. Notable reporting to the chief risk officer was also reported.

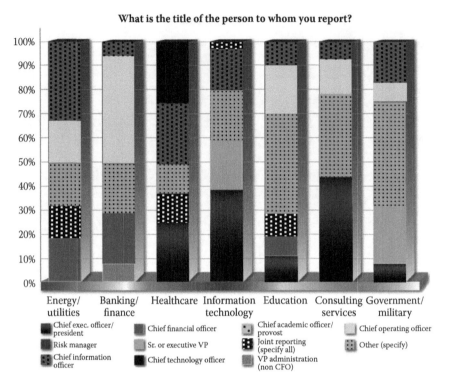

What is the title of the person to whom you report?

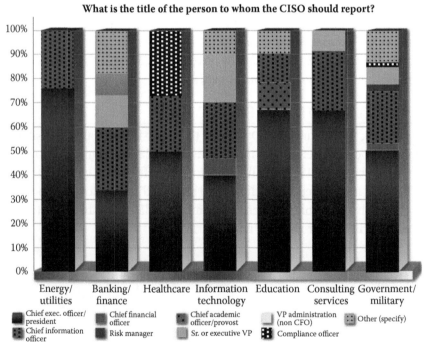

What is the title of the person to whom the CISO should report?

A very important finding from our primary research is the fact that the majority of respondents report to the corporated board.

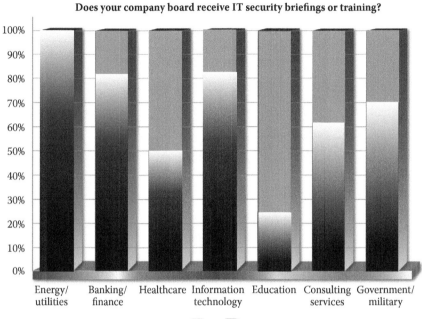

Does your company board receive IT security briefings or training?

4.5 ABILITY TO ENFORCE COMPLIANCE

CISOs have a great responsibility, and 75% note that they also have authority to enforce compliance with their IT organization's security policy. On the basis of the data, however, most in government do not.

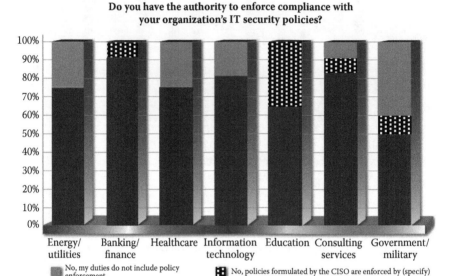

Do you have the authority to enforce compliance with your organization's IT security policies?

4.6 METHOD THAT BEST PREPARES SOMEONE TO BECOME A CISO

In addition to core training and certification, Certified Information Systems Security Professional (CISSP) is considered the gold standard, and CISOs appreciate and need mentoring and coaching by other CISOs to successfully execute the role. Without it, the respondents note the significance of on-the-job training, with 27% (second highest response) considering on-the-job training as the best method for preparation.

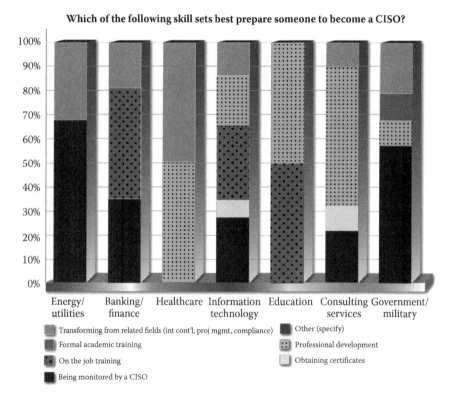

Which of the following skill sets best prepare someone to become a CISO?

4.7 CYBERATTACKS: A MAJOR THREAT TO INDUSTRY

Almost all (95%) cybersecurity professionals note that cyberattacks continue to be a significant threat to the business.

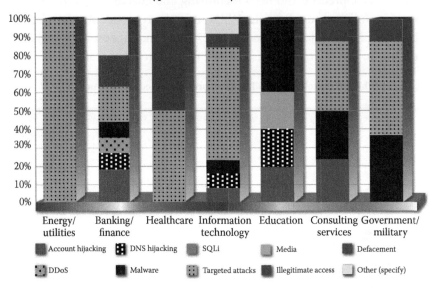

Which type of attack are you most concerned with?

4.8 TOP FIVE IT/CYBERSECURITY PRIORITIES IN THE NEXT 12 MONTHS

Risk management, regulatory compliance, and application vulnerabilities are the top three CISO priorities in 2016. It is interesting to note that application code review and development of application security infrastructure are both near the bottom.

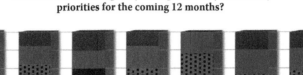

Which of the following are your top five IT/cybersecurity priorities for the coming 12 months?

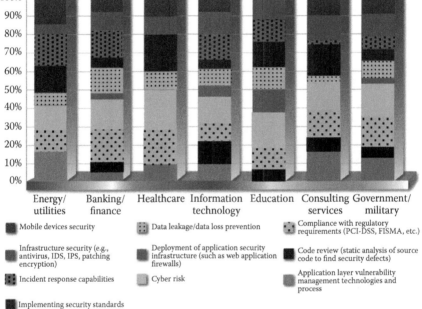

4.9 WHICH SECURITY STANDARDS/ FRAMEWORKS ARE MOST EFFECTIVE?

CISOs are receiving security guidance on standards and frameworks from a wide variety of sources. More than 50% are consulting National Institute of Standards and Technology (NIST) guidance (800-xx), 45% from Information Technology Infrastructure Library (ITIL) documentation, and 43% from International Organization for Standardization/ International Electrotechnical Commission (ISO/IEC) standards. Noteworthy is that more than 29 different cybersecurity sources are being regularly used by CISOs.

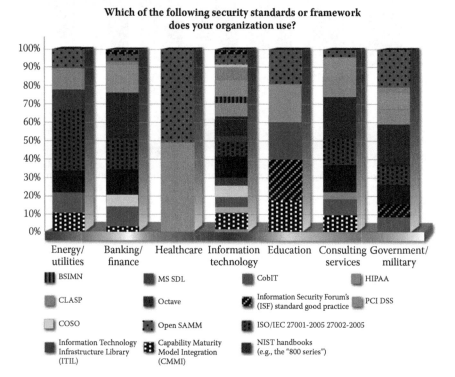

Which of the following security standards or framework does your organization use?

4.10 WORKFORCE AND TALENT

The vast majority of reporting CISOs are white (64%), male, and 50 years or older, with 2% being 30 years or younger. This suggests that workforce and talent issues in the key role will be a top priority for HR professionals of every industry vertical.

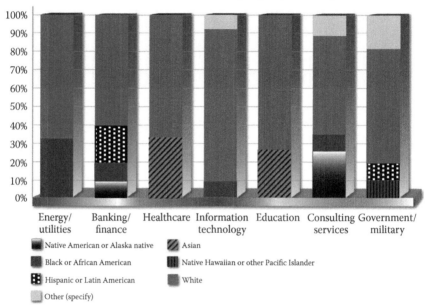

Within which racial/ethnic group do you identify?

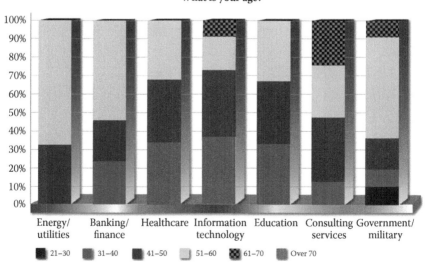

What is your age?

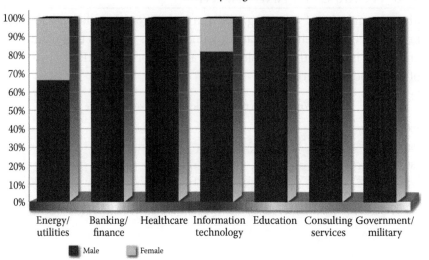

CHAPTER 5

Cloud Computing

CLOUD COMPUTING IS A model for enabling ubiquitous, convenient, on-demand network access to a shared pool of configurable computing resources (e.g., networks, servers, storage, applications, and services) that can be rapidly provisioned and released with minimal management effort or service provider interaction. This model is the most recent evolution of information technology (IT) that began with a focus on big infrastructure—mainframes, big point-to-point networks, centralized databases, and big batch jobs. Toward the end, terminals evolved into personal computers, networks went from hierarchical—with the mainframes at the center of each network—to decentralized, with a broader, generally more numerous collection of servers and storage scattered throughout an organization. While batch work still existed, many programs became interactive through this age, eventually gaining much more visual interfaces along the way.

Infrastructure tended to be associated with particular applications—a practice since pejoratively known as "application silos"—and important applications generally demanded enterprise-grade (read expensive) infrastructure ... mainframes or big servers, and so forth. This period also saw the rise of the databases, along with the beginnings of specialized storage infrastructure upon which those databases relied.

5.1 RISE OF THE INTERNET

Development and near ubiquity of easy-to-use, visually attractive devices, devices that could be used by nearly everyone led to the rise of the Internet—Sun, Cisco, Mosaic (which became) Netscape, web 1.0, eBay, Yahoo, baby.com, and the first Internet bubble. The biggest technical contribution of the second age was in the network itself. In being forced to deal with the possibility of massive network failures caused by a nuclear attack, researchers endowed their invention with the ability to self-organize, to seek out alternate routes for traffic, and to adapt to all sorts of unforeseen circumstances. The single point of failure that was typical of mainframe-inspired networks was removed and the biggest technological barrier to scaling went away.

5.2 THE TRANSFORMATION

This is when Yahoo started "indexing the Internet," which, for some time, was mostly manually constructed. While this was sufficient for a while, it soon became apparent that manually built indices could never keep up with the growth of the Internet itself. Several other indexing efforts began—including AltaVista, Google, and others—but it was Google where everything came together. This was the birth of Cloud Computing.

5.3 KEY CHARACTERISTICS OF CLOUD COMPUTING

Google and soon thereafter Amazon Web Services leverage five key characteristics in the development of unique industry business models. As defined by the US National Institute of Standards and Technology (NIST), these essential characteristics were as follows:

Rapid Elasticity: Elasticity is defined as the ability to scale resources both up and down as needed. To the consumer, the cloud appears to be infinite, and the consumer can purchase as much or as little computing power as they need. This is one of the essential characteristics of Cloud Computing in the NIST definition.

Measured Service: Aspects of the cloud service are controlled and monitored by the cloud provider. This is crucial for billing, access control, resource optimization, capacity planning, and other tasks. Cloud systems automatically control and optimize resource use by leveraging a metering capability at some level of abstraction appropriate to the type of service (e.g., storage, processing, bandwidth, and active user accounts). Resource usage can be monitored, controlled, and reported, providing transparency for both the provider and consumer of the utilized service.

On-Demand Self-Service: The on-demand and self-service aspects of Cloud Computing mean that a consumer can use cloud services as needed without any human interaction with the cloud provider.

Ubiquitous Network Access (Broad Network Access): The cloud provider's capabilities are available over the network and can be accessed through standard mechanisms by both thick and thin clients (e.g., mobile phones, laptops, and personal digital assistants).

Resource Pooling: It allows a cloud provider to serve its consumers via a multitenant model. Physical and virtual resources are assigned and reassigned according to consumer demand. There is a sense of location independence in that the customer generally has no control or knowledge over the exact location of the provided resources but may be able to specify location at a higher level of abstraction (e.g., country, state, or data center). Examples of resources include storage, processing, memory, network bandwidth, and virtual machines (VMs).

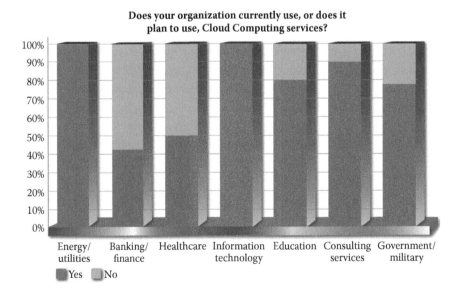

Does your organization currently use, or does it plan to use, Cloud Computing services?

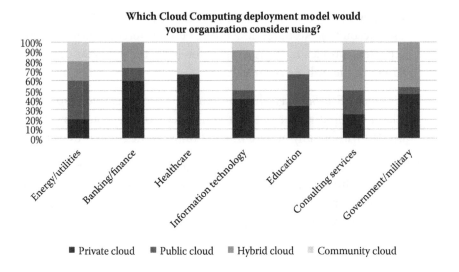

5.4 CLOUD COMPUTING DEPLOYMENT MODELS

As the unique aspects of cloud became apparent, four cloud deployment models were also identified—public cloud, private cloud, hybrid cloud, and community cloud (Figure 5.1).

5.4.1 Public Cloud

In simple terms, public cloud services are characterized as being available to clients from a third-party service provider via the Internet. The term *public* does not always mean free, although it can be free or fairly inexpensive to use. A public cloud does not mean that a user's data are publicly visible; public cloud vendors typically provide an access control mechanism for their users. Public clouds provide an elastic, cost-effective means to deploy solutions.

Although many organizations use public clouds for private business benefit, they do not control how those cloud services are operated, accessed, or secured. Popular examples of public clouds include Amazon Elastic Compute Cloud (EC2), Google Apps, and Salesforce.com.

Many organizations have adopted different cloud models simultaneously, leading to a hybrid cloud environment in which some IT assets and services are hosted in internal clouds while others are delivered through externally hosted private clouds and public clouds.

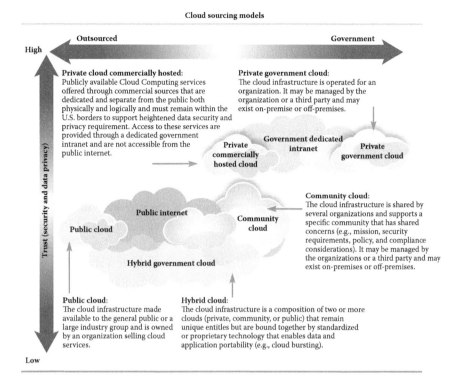

FIGURE 5.1   Cloud sourcing models.

5.4.2 Benefits of Public Clouds

Public cloud benefits include the following:

- Reduce computing costs

- Reduce infrastructure footprint

- Achieve a more flexible computing environment

- Map capacity to demand (no under- or overprovisioning—buy only what is needed)

- Decouple applications from infrastructure constraints

- Ensure capacity is there when you need it

5.4.3 Private Cloud

Private cloud describes an IT infrastructure in which a shared pool of computing resources—servers, networks, storage, applications, and software services—can be rapidly provisioned, dynamically allocated, and operated for the benefit of a single organization. A private cloud offers many of the benefits of a public Cloud Computing environment, such as being elastic and service based. The difference between a private cloud and a public cloud is that in a private cloud–based service, data and processes are managed within the organization without the restrictions of network bandwidth, security exposures, and legal requirements that using public cloud services might entail. In addition, private cloud services offer the provider and the user greater control of the cloud infrastructure, improving security and resiliency because user access and the networks used are restricted and designated.

Private cloud describes an IT infrastructure in which a shared pool of computing resources—servers, networks, storage, applications, and software services—can be rapidly provisioned, dynamically allocated, and operated for the benefit of a single organization. Private clouds are similar in many ways to the traditional IT service delivery model, with three key differences:

1. IT resources are virtualized, leading to much more efficient use and flexible allocation. Most notably, virtualization enables the dynamic transfer or sharing of services within the cloud infrastructure and the secure partitioning of services for multitenancy. "Tenants" sharing a server or application can be either completely different companies in an external cloud scenario or different business functions or groups within internal clouds.

2. The organization need not physically own or operate the IT assets that form its private cloud. Some assets can be outsourced to cloud providers: for instance, outside data centers may be leased to run specific applications. Nevertheless, the organization still effectively "owns" its private cloud by controlling and setting policies governing how virtual IT assets are operated, with cloud vendors guaranteeing specific levels of service and conformance to agreed-upon standards for information security and compliance.

3. Within a virtualized environment, just about everything can be measured, including CPU cycles and bits transmitted. As a result, clouds can be monitored at a highly granular level beyond the typical latency- and performance-based measurements of traditional IT

environments. This opens up the potential for usage-based billing or charge-backs, something that is already common with public cloud services, such as Amazon EC2.

Internal clouds are a type of private cloud in which all aspects of IT service delivery are physically owned and operated by the organization itself. In terms of monitoring and proving compliance with information policies, organizations presumably have complete visibility, transparency, and control over their internal clouds, because they own and maintain the entire cloud infrastructure, from servers to services.

5.4.4 Benefits of Private Clouds

Benefits of private clouds include the following:

- Reduce total cost of ownership (TCO) for operating infrastructure—hardware, power, cooling

- Increase return on investment (ROI) on existing hardware

- Achieve a more flexible computing environment

- Map capacity to demand (no under- or overprovisioning—buy only what is needed)

- Automate manual provisioning tasks

- Decouple applications from infrastructure constraints

- Ensure capacity is there when you need it

5.4.5 Hybrid Cloud

A hybrid cloud is a combination of a public and private cloud that interoperates. In this model, users typically outsource nonbusiness-critical information and processing to the public cloud, while keeping business-critical services and data in their control.

5.4.6 Benefits of Hybrid Clouds

Benefits of hybrid clouds include the following:

- Achieve a more flexible computing environment

- Reduce computing costs

- Achieve a more flexible computing environment

- Map capacity to demand (no under- or overprovisioning—buy only what is needed)

- Automate manual provisioning tasks

- Decouple applications from infrastructure constraints

- Ensure capacity is there when you need it

5.4.7 Community Cloud

A community cloud is controlled and used by a group of organizations that have shared interests, such as specific security requirements or a common mission. The members of the community share access to the data and applications in the cloud.

5.5 CLOUD COMPUTING SERVICE MODELS

This new model for the delivery and consumption of IT quickly coalesced around three commodity services:

- Software as a Service (SaaS)—The consumer uses an application but does not control the operating system, hardware, or network infrastructure on which it is running. Example: Salesforce.com.

- Platform as a Service (PaaS)—The consumer uses a hosting environment for their applications. The consumer controls the applications that run in the environment (and possibly has some control over the hosting environment) but does not control the operating system, hardware, or network infrastructure on which they are running. The platform is typically an application framework. Examples: Google App Engine, Force.com.

- Infrastructure as a Service (IaaS)—The consumer uses "fundamental computing resources" such as processing power, storage, networking components, or middleware. The consumer can control the operating system, storage, deployed applications, and possibly networking components such as firewalls and load balancers, but not the cloud infrastructure beneath them. Example: Amazon played a key role in the development of Cloud Computing by modernizing their data centers after the dot-com bubble, which, like most computer networks, used as little as 10% of their capacity at any one time just to leave room for occasional spikes. Having found that the new cloud architecture resulted in significant internal efficiency improvements whereby small, fast-moving "two-pizza teams" could add new features faster and easier, Amazon started providing access to their systems through Amazon Web Services on a utility computing basis in 2005. This characterization of the genesis of Amazon Web Services has been characterized as an extreme oversimplification by a technical contributor to the Amazon Web Services project.

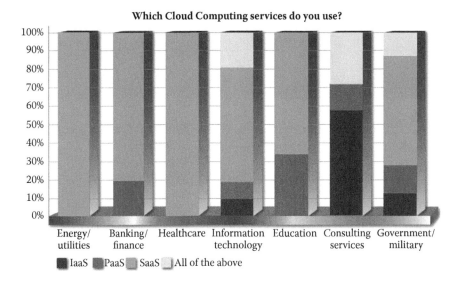

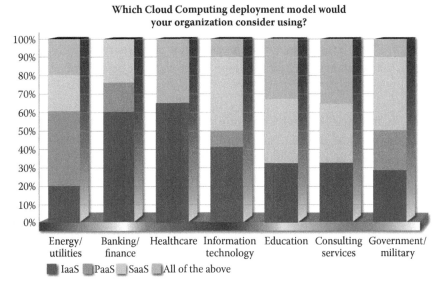

Although there was some initial confusion with similar computing models such as "Grid Computing" and "Utility Computing," the market soon settled on these as standard cloud service models.

What is Cloud Computing Lecture (https://oncloud.talentlms.com/unit /view/id:1757)

5.6 GENERAL CLOUD COMPUTING BENEFITS

Cloud Computing represents a natural maturation of IT as a utility service. Using water as an example, there was a time when every household, town, farm, or village had its own water well. Today, shared public utilities give us access to clean water by simply turning on the tap. Just like the water from the tap in your kitchen, Cloud Computing services can be turned on or off quickly as needed. Similar to the water company, there is a team of dedicated professionals making sure the service provided is safe and available on a 24/7 basis. Also, when the tap is not on, you are not only saving water, you are not paying for the resource as well. The benefits of cloud are many (Figure 5.2):

- Economical—Cloud Computing has also turned out to be a very economical model. Using this model, commodity IT services are available at a fraction of the cost of traditional IT services. This can eliminate upfront capital expenditures and dramatically reduce administrative burdens. Cloud Computing is a pay-as-you-go approach to IT, in which a low initial investment is required to get going. Additional investment is incurred as system use increases and costs can decrease if usage decreases. In this way, cash flows better match total system cost.

FIGURE 5.2 Cloud Computing benefits lecture. (From https://oncloud.talentlms
.com/unit/view/id:1737.)

- Flexible—Cloud is also flexible in that IT departments that anticipate fluctuations in user load do not have to scramble to secure additional hardware and software. With Cloud Computing, they can add and subtract capacity as its network load dictates, and pay only for what they use. Cloud Computing provides on-demand computing across technologies, business solutions, and large ecosystems of providers, reducing time to implement new solutions from months to days.

- Rapid implementation—Without the need to go through the procurement and certification processes, and with a near-limitless selection of services, tools, and features, Cloud Computing helps projects get off the ground in record time.

- Consistent service—Network outages can send an IT department scrambling for answers. Cloud Computing can offer a higher level of service and reliability, and an immediate response to emergency situations.

- Increased effectiveness—Cloud Computing frees the user from the finer details of IT system configuration and maintenance, enabling them to spend more time on mission-critical tasks and less time on IT operations and maintenance.

- Energy efficient—Because resources are pooled, each user community does not need to have its own dedicated IT infrastructure. Several groups can share computing resources, leading to higher utilization rates, fewer servers, and less energy consumption.

- Access anywhere—You are no longer tethered to a single computer or network. You can change computers or move to portable devices, and your existing applications and documents follow you through the cloud.

- Elastic scalability and pay-as-you-go—Add and subtract capacity as your needs change. Pay for only what you use.

- Easy to implement—You do not need to purchase hardware, software licenses, or implementation services.

- Service quality—Cloud service providers offer reliable services, large storage and computing capacity, and 24/7 service and uptime.

- Delegate noncritical applications—Cloud Computing provides a way to outsource noncritical applications to service providers, allowing agency IT resources to focus on business-critical applications.

- Always the latest software—You are no longer faced with choosing between obsolete software and high upgrade costs. When the applications are web based, updates are automatic and are available the next time you log into the cloud.

- Sharing documents and group collaboration—Cloud Computing lets you access all your applications and documents from anywhere in the world, freeing you from the confines of the desktop and facilitating group collaboration on documents and projects.

5.7 CLOUD USE CASES

As the adoption of cloud accelerated, recognizable patterns and use cases soon emerged. These use cases also shared. Typical use case examples were as follows:

- **End user to cloud**—In this scenario, an end user is accessing data or applications in the cloud. Common applications of this type include e-mail hosting and social networking sites. A user of Gmail, Facebook, or LinkedIn accesses the application and their data through any browser on any device. The user does not want to keep up with anything more than a password; their data are stored and managed in the cloud. Most importantly, the user has no idea how the underlying architecture works. If they can get to the Internet, they can get to their data.

- **Enterprise to cloud to end user**—In this scenario, an enterprise is using the cloud to deliver data and services to the end user. When the end user interacts with the enterprise, the enterprise accesses the cloud to retrieve data or manipulate it, sending the results to the end user. The end user can be someone within the enterprise or an external customer.

- **Enterprise to cloud**—This use case involves an enterprise using cloud services for its internal processes. This might be the most common use case in the early stages of Cloud Computing because it gives the enterprise the most control. In this scenario, the enterprise uses cloud services to supplement the resources it needs.

- **Enterprise to cloud to enterprise**—This use case involves two enterprises using the same cloud. The focus here is hosting resources in the cloud so that applications from the enterprises can interoperate. A supply chain is the most obvious example for this use case.

- **Changing cloud vendors**—This use case involves working with a different cloud vendor, either adding an additional vendor or replacing an existing one. It applies to all of the other use cases discussed in this paper. Being able to work with other vendors without major changes is one of the main benefits of openness and standardization. There are four different scenarios here, each of which has slightly different requirements.

  - **Scenario 1**: Changing SaaS vendors—In this scenario, a cloud customer changes SaaS vendors. Both SaaS vendors provide the same application (CRM, accounting, word processing, etc.). Documents and data created with one vendor's software should be importable by the second vendor's software. In some cases, the customer might need to use the two vendors interchangeably.

  - **Scenario 2**: Changing middleware vendors—In this scenario, a cloud customer changes cloud middleware vendors. Existing data, queries, message queues, and applications must be exportable from one vendor and importable by the other.

- **Scenario 3**: Changing cloud storage vendors—In this scenario, a cloud customer changes cloud storage vendors.

- **Scenario 4**: Changing VM hosts—In this scenario, a cloud customer wants to take VMs built on one cloud vendor's system and run it on another cloud vendor's system.

The industry also soon discovered a list of repeatable technical and operational requirements:

- **Identity**: The cloud service must authenticate the end user.

- **Open client**: Access to the cloud service should not require a particular platform or technology.

- **Security**: Security (including privacy) is a common requirement to all use cases, although the details of those requirements will vary widely from one use case to the next. Any use case involving an enterprise will have more sophisticated security requirements than one involving a single end user. Similarly, the more advanced enterprise use cases to follow will have equally more advanced security requirements.

- **Service level agreements (SLAs) and benchmarks**: Although SLAs for end users will usually be much simpler than those for enterprises, cloud vendors must be clear about what guarantees of service they provide. In addition to the basic SLAs required by end users, enterprises who sign contracts based on SLAs will need a standard way of benchmarking performance. There must be an unambiguous way of defining what a cloud provider will deliver, and there must be an unambiguous way of measuring what was actually delivered.

- **Federated identity**: In addition to the basic identity needed by an end user, an enterprise user is likely to have an identity with the enterprise. The ideal is that the enterprise user manages a single ID, with an infrastructure federating other identities that might be required by cloud services.

- **Location awareness**: Depending on the kind of data the enterprise is managing on the user's behalf, there might be legal restrictions on the location of the physical server where the data are stored. Although this violates the Cloud Computing ideal that the user should not have to know details of the physical infrastructure, this requirement is essential. Many applications cannot be moved to the cloud until cloud vendors provide an API for determining the location of the physical hardware that delivers the cloud service.

- **Metering and monitoring**: All cloud services must be metered and monitored for cost control, charge-backs, and provisioning.

- **Management and governance**: Public cloud providers make it very easy to open an account and begin using cloud services; such ease of use creates the risk that individuals in an enterprise will use cloud services on their own initiative. Management of VMs and of cloud services such as storage, databases, and message queues is needed to track what services are used. Governance is crucial to ensure that policies and government regulations are followed wherever Cloud Computing is used. Other governance requirements will be industry and geography specific.

- **Common file format for VMs**: A VM created for one cloud vendor's platform should be portable to another vendor's platform. Any solution to this requirement must account for differences in the ways cloud vendors attach storage to VMs.

- **Common APIs for cloud storage and middleware**: The enterprise use cases require common APIs for access to cloud storage services, cloud databases, and other cloud middleware services such as message queues. Writing custom code that works only for a particular vendor's cloud service locks the enterprise into that vendor's system and eliminates some of the financial benefits and flexibility that Cloud Computing provides.

- **Data and application federation**: Enterprise applications need to combine data from multiple cloud-based sources, and they need to coordinate the activities of applications running in different clouds.

- **Life cycle management**: Enterprises must be able to manage the life cycle of applications and documents. This requirement includes versioning of applications and the retention and destruction of data. Discovery is a major issue for many organizations. There are substantial legal liabilities if certain data are no longer available. In addition to data retention, in some cases, an enterprise will want to make sure data are destroyed at some point.

- **Transactions and concurrency**: For applications and data shared by different enterprises, transactions and concurrency are vital. If two enterprises are using the same cloud-hosted application, VM, middleware, or storage, it is important that any changes made by either enterprise are done reliably.

- **Interoperability**: Because more than one enterprise is involved, interoperability between the enterprises is essential.

- **Industry-specific standards**: Moving documents and data from one vendor's application to another requires both applications to support common formats. The formats involved will depend on the type of application.

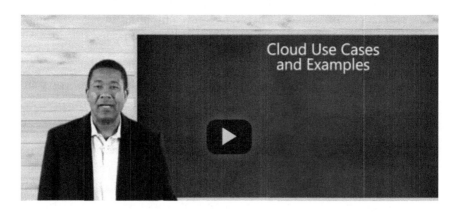

Video Lecture: Use Cases and Examples (https://oncloud.talentlms.com /unit/view/id:1758)

5.8 CLOUD COMPUTING TECHNOLOGIES

5.8.1 Commodity Hardware

Chips (processors, memory, etc.), storage (mostly disc drives), and network (within a data center, wide area, and wireless)—there have been large strides made in the capabilities of what is—by historical standards—throwaway equipment.

For example, a company was able to match a competitor's industry-leading, mainframe-based performance in processing high-volume customer transaction with less than a dozen cheap commodity boxes sitting on a repurposed kitchen rack. Total bill? Less than $10,000. Yes it works, and it works very well. The key, of course, was in how the applications were constructed and how that set of machines is reliably managed.

5.8.2 Network Speed

While network performance has not increased at the same rate as either processor or storage performance, huge strides have been made in both the connections within a data center and those outside. For example, a "gigE" network card (for use by a commodity computer within a data center) will be less than $10 each in small quantities. To put that in perspective, that is approximately 400% faster than the internal bus connections (the key internal connectivity within server computers) of the typical "big servers" of the early 1980s.

A 10-Mbps wired connection for the home or office will average less than $50 per month in the United States, and even less than that in many parts of the world. Mainstream mobile wireless speeds will be closer to 7 Mbps, at the cost of only a modest part of the typical monthly cell phone budget. The point is simple: whether within the data center, at fixed locations throughout the world, or on mobile devices, cheap, fast, reliable, and ubiquitous network connections are a fact of life.

5.8.3 Pervasive High-Quality Access

The reality—quality, variety, quantity—of high-quality, visually attractive, widely available devices has had a tremendous impact on the development of Cloud Computing. Typical devices include fixed desktops with one or more flat panels; laptops and netbooks of every size, price range, and performance; and ubiquitous, sometimes specialized, nearly always relatively inexpensive handheld devices such as the iPhone and its growing range of competitors. All these devices share in common a wide range of wireless high-speed Internet access.

This plethora of high-quality, pervasive devices have greatly increased the number of customers for services and content—the data and applications sold on the cloud—as well as the appetite for even more services and data. In March 2008, Apple announced that they would create a marketplace from which third-party developers could sell applications to owners of an iPhone. Despite a tremendous amount of uncertainty—including many who thought that the whole concept would simply fizzle out for any of a number of reasons—within the first 9 months, Apple was able to sell more than 1 billion individual applications. From zero to a billion in less than a year.

5.8.4 Data Storage Architectures

Object storage (also known as *object-based storage*) is a storage architecture that manages data as objects. Each object typically includes the data itself, a variable amount of metadata, and a globally unique identifier. Object storage can be implemented at multiple levels, including the device level (object storage device), the system level, and the interface level. In each case, object storage seeks to enable capabilities not addressed by other storage architectures, like interfaces that can be directly programmable by the application, a namespace that can span multiple instances of physical hardware, and data management functions like data replication and data distribution at object-level granularity. Object storage systems allow relatively inexpensive, scalable, and self-healing retention of massive amounts of unstructured data and are typically used by cloud service providers.

Block storage—a block, sometimes called a physical record, is a sequence of bytes or bits, usually containing some whole number of records, having a maximum length, a *block size*. Data thus structured are said to be *blocked*. The process of putting data into blocks is called *blocking*, while *deblocking* is the process of extracting data from blocks. Blocked data are normally stored in a data buffer and read or written a whole block at a time. Blocking reduces the overhead and speeds up the handling of the data stream. Most file systems are based on a block device, which is a level of abstraction for the hardware responsible for storing and retrieving specified blocks of data, though the block size in file systems may be a multiple of the physical block size. Block storage is normally abstracted by a file system or database management system for use by applications and end users.

File system (or filesystem) is used to control how data are stored and retrieved. Without a file system, information placed in a storage area would be one large body of data with no way to tell where one piece of information stops and the next begins. By separating the data into individual pieces, and giving each piece a name, the information is easily separated and identified. Taking its name from the way paper-based information systems are named, each group of data is called a "file." The structure and logic rules used to manage the groups of information and their names are called a "file system."

Data model organizes data elements and standardizes how the data elements relate to one another. Since data elements document real-life people, places, and things and the events between them, the data model represents reality; for example, a house has many windows or a cat has two eyes. Computers are used for the accounting of these real-life things and events and therefore the data model is a necessary standard to ensure exact communication between human beings. Structured data adhere to a given data model.

Unstructured data (or **unstructured information**) refer to information that either does not have a predefined data model or is not organized in a predefined manner. Unstructured information is typically text heavy but may contain data such as dates, numbers, and facts as well. This results in irregularities and ambiguities that make it difficult to understand using traditional computer programs as compared to data stored in fielded form in databases or annotated (semantically tagged) in documents.

Semistructured data are a form of structured data that do not conform with the formal structure of data models associated with relational databases or other forms of data tables, but nonetheless contain tags or other markers to separate semantic elements and enforce hierarchies of records and fields within the data. Therefore, it is also known as self-describing structure. In the semistructured data, the entities belonging to the same class may have different attributes although they are grouped together, and the attributes' order is not important. Semistructured data are increasingly occurring since the advent of the Internet where full-text documents and databases are not the only forms of data anymore and different applications need a medium for exchanging information. In object-oriented databases, one often finds semistructured data.

A graph data structure consists of a finite (and possibly mutable) set of **nodes** or **vertices**, together with a set of ordered pairs of these nodes (or, in some cases, a set of unordered pairs). These pairs are known as **edges** or **arcs**. As in mathematics, an edge (x,y) is said to **point** or **go from** x to y. The nodes may be part of the graph structure, or may be external entities represented by integer indices or references. A graph data structure may also associate to each edge some **edge value**, such as a symbolic label or a numeric attribute (cost, capacity, length, etc.).

Document-oriented database is a computer program designed for storing, retrieving, and managing document-oriented information, also known as semistructured data. Document-oriented databases are one of the main categories of NoSQL databases and the popularity of the term *document-oriented database* (or *document store*) has grown with the use of the term NoSQL itself.

The first two ages of computing have very much been dominated by the database systems, often relational databases such as Oracle, MySQL, SQLServer, Postgress, and others. Entire (data management) organizations exist in most enterprises to manage the structure of this relational data within these repositories, with strict rules about how such data are accessed, updated, and so forth.

Unfortunately, what we have learned from abundant experience is that, at some point, the block to scaling any given application will nearly always be the relational database itself.

As a result, the whole approach to reliably storing, processing, and managing data at large scale has been changed, resulting in approaches like Hadoop and MapReduce, which use parallel processing in cloud-based platforms in order to enable rapid management and access to unstructured data stores.

5.8.5 Data Centers

A data center is a facility used to house computer systems and associated components, such as telecommunications and storage systems. It generally includes redundant or backup power supplies, redundant data communications connections, environmental controls (e.g., air conditioning, fire suppression), and various security devices.

A data center can occupy one room of a building, one or more floors, or an entire building. Most of the equipment is often in the form of servers mounted in 19-inch rack cabinets, which are usually placed in single rows forming corridors (so-called aisles) between them. This allows people access to the front and rear of each cabinet. Servers differ greatly in size from 1U servers to large freestanding storage silos that occupy many square feet of floor space. Some equipment such as mainframe computers and storage devices are often as big as the racks themselves and are placed alongside them. Very large data centers may use shipping containers packed with 1000 or more servers each; when repairs or upgrades are needed, whole containers are replaced (rather than repairing individual servers).

Availability expectations—The higher the availability needs of a data center, the higher the capital and operational costs of building and managing it. Business needs should dictate the level of availability required and should be evaluated based on characterization of the criticality of IT systems' estimated cost analyses from modeled scenarios. In other words, how can an appropriate level of availability best be met by design criteria to avoid financial and operational risks as a result of downtime? If the estimated cost of downtime within a specified time unit exceeds the amortized capital costs and operational expenses, a higher level of availability should be factored into the data center design. If the cost of avoiding downtime greatly exceeds the cost of downtime itself, a lower level of availability should be factored into the design.

Location—Aspects such as proximity to available power grids, telecommunications infrastructure, networking services, transportation lines, and emergency services can affect costs, risk, security, and other factors to be taken into consideration for data center design. Location affects data center design as well because the climatic conditions dictate what cooling technologies should be deployed. In turn, this affects uptime and the costs associated with cooling. For example, the topology and the cost of managing a data center in a warm, humid climate will vary greatly from managing one in a cool, dry climate.

Security—Physical security also plays a large role with data centers. Physical access to the site is usually restricted to selected personnel, with controls including bollards and mantraps. Video camera surveillance and permanent security guards are almost always present if the data center is large or contains sensitive information on any of the systems within. The use of fingerprint recognition mantraps is starting to be commonplace.

Multiple data centers are used in Cloud Computing implementations in order to enhance availability. Locations are typically 500–1000 miles apart and on separate electrical power grids.

5.8.6 Virtualization

Virtualization is the ability to operate particular resources (such as computers, networks, etc.) largely independent of the physical infrastructure upon which they are deployed.

It started as a way to share the use of very expensive mainframes between otherwise incompatible operating systems and then flowed into the later but similar trend to consolidate large numbers of small servers (each typically dedicated to one or two specific applications).

This can be a tremendous boon for operations. For example, the initial configuration of the operating system for a server, along with the applications to run on that server, can take hours if not days. With virtualization, that initial work is done once and the results are put on the shelf, to be deployed onto physical hardware when needed. This process, sometimes referred to as "hydration," can be done in as little as a few seconds to minutes and repeated as often as needed, thereby enabling the possibility of easily deploying basic software to large numbers of computers.

Each user has a single view of the available resources, independently of how they are arranged in terms of physical devices. Virtualization advantages also include high availability, continuity (fault tolerance), security, scaling, cloning, and mobility.

Important virtualization terms include the following:

- A **VM** is an emulation of a particular computer system. VMs operate on the basis of the computer architecture and functions of a real or hypothetical computer, and their implementations may involve specialized hardware, software, or a combination of both.

- A **VM image template** is a perfect, model copy of a VM from which you can clone, convert, or deploy more VMs.

- A **virtual private server** (**VPS**) is a VM sold as a service by an Internet hosting service. A VPS runs its own copy of an operating system, and customers have superuser-level access to that operating system instance, so they can install almost any software that runs on that operating system.

- A **virtual appliance** is a preconfigured VM image, ready to run on a hypervisor; virtual appliances are a subset of the broader class of software appliances. Installation of a software appliance on a VM and packaging that into an image create a virtual appliance. Like software appliances, virtual appliances are intended to eliminate the installation, configuration, and maintenance costs associated with running complex stacks of software.

5.8.7 Hypervisor

A **hypervisor** or **virtual machine monitor** is a piece of computer software, firmware, or hardware that creates and runs VMs.

A computer on which a hypervisor is running one or more VMs is defined as a *host machine*. Each VM is called a *guest machine*. The hypervisor presents the guest operating systems with a virtual operating platform and manages the execution of the guest operating systems. Multiple instances of a variety of operating systems may share the virtualized hardware resources.

- Type 1: native or bare-metal hypervisors—These hypervisors run directly on the host's hardware to control the hardware and to manage guest operating systems. For this reason, they are sometimes called bare metal hypervisors. A guest operating system runs as a process on the host.

- Type 2: hosted hypervisors—These hypervisors run on a conventional operating system just as other computer programs do. Type 2 hypervisors abstract guest operating systems from the host operating system. VMware Workstation and VirtualBox are examples of type 2 hypervisors.

Although virtualization is not a mandatory element of cloud, its use has become pervasive. Some important uses of this technology follow.

5.8.8 Hardware Virtualization Types

Full virtualization—almost complete simulation of the actual hardware to allow software, which typically consists of a guest operating system, to run unmodified.

Partial virtualization—some but not all of the target environment is simulated. Some guest programs, therefore, may need modifications to run in this virtual environment.

Paravirtualization—a hardware environment is not simulated; however, the guest programs are executed in their own isolated domains, as if they are running on a separate system. Guest programs need to be specifically modified to run in this environment.

Hardware-assisted virtualization is a platform virtualization approach that enables efficient full virtualization using help from hardware capabilities, primarily from the host processors. Hardware-assisted virtualization is also known as **accelerated virtualization**; Xen calls it **hardware virtual machine**, and Virtual Iron calls it **native virtualization**.

5.8.9 Desktop Virtualization

Desktop virtualization is the concept of separating the logical desktop from the physical machine.

One form of desktop virtualization, virtual desktop infrastructure (VDI), can be thought of as a more advanced form of hardware virtualization. Rather than interacting with a host computer directly via a keyboard, mouse, and monitor, the user interacts with the host computer using another desktop computer or a mobile device by means of a network connection, such as a LAN, Wireless LAN, or even the Internet. In addition, the host computer in this scenario becomes a server computer capable of hosting multiple VMs at the same time for multiple users.

Another form, session virtualization, allows multiple users to connect and log into a shared but powerful computer over the network and use it simultaneously. Each is given a desktop and a personal folder in which they store their files.

Thin clients, which are seen in desktop virtualization, are simple and/or cheap computers that are primarily designed to connect to the network. They may lack significant hard disk storage space, RAM, or even processing power, but many organizations are beginning to look at the cost benefits of eliminating "thick client" desktops that are packed with software (and require software licensing fees) and making more strategic investments. Desktop virtualization simplifies software versioning and patch management, where the new image is simply updated on the server, and the desktop gets the updated version when it reboots. It also enables centralized control over what applications the user is allowed to have access to on the workstation.

Moving virtualized desktops into the cloud creates hosted virtual desktops, where the desktop images are centrally managed and maintained by a specialist hosting firm. Benefits include scalability and the reduction of capital expenditure, which is replaced by a monthly operational cost.

5.8.10 Software Virtualization

Operating system–level virtualization denotes hosting of multiple virtualized environments within a single operating system instance.

Linux Containers (LXC) is an operating system–level virtualization method for running multiple isolated Linux systems (containers) on a single control host. The Linux kernel comprises cgroups for resource isolation (CPU, memory, block I/O, network, etc.) that does not require starting any VMs. Cgroups also provides namespace isolation to completely isolate applications' view of the operating environment, including process trees, network, user ids, and mounted file systems. LXC combines cgroups and namespace support to provide an isolated environment for applications. Docker can also use LXC as one of its execution drivers, enabling image management and providing deployment services.

Application virtualization and workspace virtualization denote the hosting of individual applications in an environment separated from the underlying operating system. Application virtualization is closely associated with the concept of portable applications.

Service virtualization implies emulating the behavior of dependent (e.g., third-party, evolving, or not implemented) system components that are needed to exercise an application under test for development or testing purposes. Rather than virtualizing entire components, it virtualizes only specific slices of dependent behavior critical to the execution of development and testing tasks.

5.8.11 Memory Virtualization

Memory virtualization means aggregating random access memory (RAM) resources from networked systems into a single memory pool.

Virtual memory denotes giving an application program the impression that it has contiguous working memory, isolating it from the underlying physical memory implementation.

5.8.12 Storage Virtualization

Storage virtualization is the process of completely abstracting logical storage from physical storage.

Distributed file system is any file system that allows access to files from multiple hosts sharing via a computer network.

Virtual file system is an abstraction layer on top of a more concrete file system, allowing client applications to access different types of concrete file systems in a uniform way.

Storage hypervisor is the software that manages storage virtualization and combines physical storage resources into one or more flexible pools of logical storage.

Virtual disk drive is a computer program that emulates a disk drive such as a hard disk drive or optical disk drive (see comparison of disc image software).

5.8.13 Data Virtualization

Data virtualization is the presentation of data as an abstract layer, independent of underlying database systems, structures, and storage.

Database virtualization is the decoupling of the database layer, which lies between the storage and application layers within the application stack over all.

5.8.14 Network Virtualization

Network virtualization denotes the creation of a virtualized network addressing space within or across network subnets.

Virtual private network (VPN) is a network protocol that replaces the actual wire or other physical media in a network with an abstract layer, allowing a network to be created over the Internet.

A **Virtual Private Cloud (VPC)** is an on-demand configurable pool of shared computing resources allocated within a **public** cloud environment, providing certain level of isolation between the different organizations (denoted as *users* hereafter) using the resources. The isolation between one VPC user and all other users of the same cloud (other VPC users as well as other public cloud users) is achieved normally through allocation of a Private IP Subnet and a virtual communication construct (such as a VLAN or a set of encrypted communication channels) per user. In a VPC solution, the previously described mechanism, providing isolation within the cloud, is accompanied with a VPN function (again, allocated per VPC user) that secures, by means of authentication and encryption, the remote access of the organization to its VPC cloud resources. With the introduction of the described isolation levels, an organization using this service is in effect working on a "**virtually private**" cloud (i.e., as if the cloud infrastructure is not shared with other organizations), and hence the name VPC. VPC is most commonly used in the context of cloud infrastructure services (IaaS). In this context, the infrastructure provider, providing the underlining public cloud infrastructure, and the provider realizing the VPC service over this infrastructure, may be different vendors.

5.8.15 Emerging Cloud Technologies

Bring your own device (BYOD), also called bring your own technology (BYOT), bring your own phone (BYOP), and bring your own PC (BYOPC), refers to the policy of permitting employees to bring personally owned mobile devices (laptops, tablets, and smartphones) to their workplace, and to use those devices to access privileged company information and applications. The term is also used to describe the same practice applied to students using personally owned devices in education settings. BYOD is making significant inroads in the business world, with approximately 75% of employees in high growth markets such as Brazil and Russia and 44% in developed markets already using their own technology at work. Surveys have indicated that businesses are unable to stop employees from bringing personal devices into the workplace. Research is divided on benefits, with some reports indicating productivity gains by employees. Companies like Workspot, Inc. believe that BYOD may help employees be more productive. Others say it increases employee morale and convenience by using their own devices and makes the company look like a flexible and attractive employer. Many feel that BYOD can even be a means to attract new hires, pointing to a survey that indicates 44% of jobseekers view an organization more positively if it supports their device.

Software Defined Everything (SDX) includes, but is not limited to, Software-defined Networking (SDN), Software-defined Data Center, Software-defined WAN, Software-defined Servers, Software-defined Services, Software-defined Storage (SDS), Software-defined IT, and so on.

Network Functions Virtualization (NFV) is a network architecture concept that proposes using IT virtualization-related technologies to virtualize entire classes of network node functions into building blocks that may be connected, or chained, together to create communication services. NFV relies on, but differs from, traditional server virtualization techniques such as those used in enterprise IT. A virtualized network function, or VNF, may consist of one or more VMs running different software and processes, on top of industry standard high-volume servers, switches and storage, or even Cloud Computing infrastructure, instead of having custom hardware appliances for each network function. For example, a virtualized session border controller function could be deployed to protect a network without the typical cost and complexity of obtaining and installing physical units. Other examples of NFV include virtualized load balancers, firewalls, intrusion detection devices, and WAN accelerators.

5.9 CLOUD ADOPTION TRENDS

Private clouds have been the first to be adopted, particularly since many organizations can realize immediate operational and cost benefits while still preserving control over the applications and information residing in their private clouds. Yet, some organizations are already looking to the next step: integrating external technology providers to further enhance the service capabilities and operational efficiency of their cloud environments. As the prospective benefits of leveraging external service providers continue to grow, many enterprise clouds will integrate outside cloud infrastructure or platform services. Some will even integrate whole public cloud services to create new hybrid models of Cloud Computing.

The rise of external service providers introduces new complexities, as well as benefits, into the delivery chain for cloud services. The leading areas of concern, according to a survey from IDG Research Services, relate to managing and safeguarding corporate information in clouds with externally hosted components. This is particularly true as information and application control moves off-premise to third-party providers. Without early planning and consideration, the evolution of more complex hybrid models could lead to the following concerning conditions, which are weighing on the minds of today's CIOs and IT professionals:

- Growth and proliferation of incompatible cloud services

- Isolation of valuable corporate information within cloud-based silos

- Escalating potential for vendor lock-in

- New complications in enforcing information security and policy compliance

If not planned for, these emerging conditions will impede the flow and value of corporate information for years to come. The main driver behind these problems is the classic challenge of information silos—the lack of cloud interoperability standards, lack of shared services that underpin multiple applications, and lack of tools to access information across applications. Like in on-premise installations, these gaps present a serious challenge in sharing information between applications and systems and even across cloud environments. Today's solutions providers are busy tackling the barriers to interoperability: embracing open standards, building shared services and creating standardized technology platforms, as well as creating APIs that help automate the integration of services across clouds.

Although solutions providers are making progress on the technology front, CIOs still see a gap between where cloud services are and where they need to be, particularly when they involve outside service providers.

While they look forward to a time when standards have evolved and cloud platforms are fully enterprise ready, they don't want to sit on the sidelines waiting for cloud maturity and lose the competitive and cost advantages of moving IT services to the cloud today. Additionally, business units in some organizations are forcing IT's hand by independently provisioning public cloud services—sealing the deal with a corporate credit card and a user terms and conditions checkbox. As a result, organizations increasingly find themselves supporting hybrid environments in which some information resides in public clouds, some resides in externally hosted private clouds, and some resides within the enterprise, either in traditional or in virtualized data centers.

The net result is that organizations are at risk of fragmenting their information architecture, isolating valuable corporate information within disparate applications and cloud services. It's not unlike the enterprise data silo problems of the 90s, when information was locked within ERP and CRM applications, requiring massive systems integration efforts. However, now, the business consequence of siloed data is more urgent: in today's climate, if you can't access and use your information, you've surrendered your business agility and lost an important competitive edge.

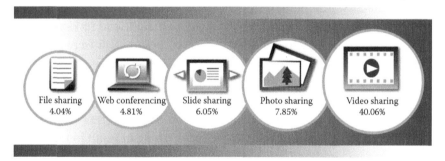

| File sharing 4.04% | Web conferencing 4.81% | Slide sharing 6.05% | Photo sharing 7.85% | Video sharing 40.06% |

Source: Creating Information Advantage in a Cloudy World,
Leadership Council for Information Advantage.

In file sharing, Dropbox and Google Drive are firmly entrenched in the top two spots, driven by consumer use. OneDrive and Box are duking it out as the top business-sponsored cloud service. The bottom half of the list remains in constant flux, with Sharefile as the one new ranking service, replacing Filefactory.

The collaboration space, which boasts the most cloud services of any category, has seen a bit of a shake-up with three new players making the

Top 10 list for the first time: Intralinks, Evernote, and ClearSlide. Most interesting, however, is the fact that Office 365 has overtaken Gmail as the top collaboration service.

In social media, the top three players (i.e., Facebook, Twitter, and LinkedIn) are constant. This quarter extends two recent trends: (1) significant movement at the bottom and (2) internationalization of social media with 4 of the top 10 sites (Sina Weibo, VK, LiveJournal, and Renren) hailing from outside the United States.

5.9.1 Data Sent to High-Risk Cloud Services

Cloud services may be considered high risk for many reasons. They may have a discouraging known-compromise history, they may permit risky behaviors such as anonymous use, they may lack basic security features such as encryption in transit and admin activity logging, and they may have sneaky terms and conditions that put your data at risk. For example, users of some popular collaboration services grant the company irrevocable and royalty-free rights to use, distribute, and otherwise exploit the content that the users upload.

These risky cloud services are a concern because they can serve as a vector for data loss, whether it is intentional or not. Last quarter, the average company uploaded 86.5 gigabytes of data to high-risk cloud services. If you look at the types of high-risk services that corporate data were going to, the top five categories were slide sharing (6.1%), file sharing (4.0%), photo sharing (7.85%), video sharing (40.1%), and web conferencing (4.81%).

In addition, nearly two-thirds of those data were sent to services that were miscategorized by URL categorization services, rendering them ungoverned by existing firewalls and proxies. This can result in the loss of corporate data and IP as well as violation of internal security policies and external regulatory requirements.

In Skyhigh's recent Cloud Adoption Risk Report of 5.9 million users and more than 175 companies, their team of researchers revealed that the number of cloud services in use was startling. The numbers ranged from a low of 97 and increased all the way up to 2154 cloud services per company with an average of 626. Even more surprising was that of the cloud services in use, only 11% had data encrypted at rest and only 4% are certified ISO 27001 compliant. These staggering numbers, along with a Forbes Leaving the Site Icon article stating that 40% of IT expenditures are done outside of the purview of the IT department and CIO's control, indicate that there is a present and growing risk to enterprises that must be brought back

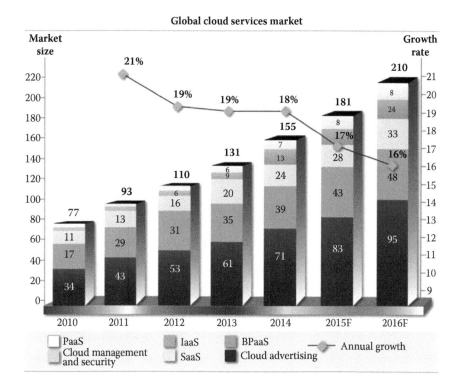

FIGURE 5.3 Cloud service market. (From http://www.consultancy.uk.)

into corporate governance and oversight for compliancy. These risks are present across all industries including the public sector, which has typically had tight controls and oversight. According to NASA's audit PDF Icon report from July of 2013, auditors found that moderate-impact systems "moved to a public cloud operated for 2 years without authorization, a security or contingency plan, or a test of the system's security controls" and reinforces the risk of unmonitored access to cloud service providers (Figure 5.3).

CHAPTER 6

Cybersecurity

6.1 INTRODUCTION

The worldwide cybersecurity market is defined by market sizing estimates that range from $71 billion in 2014 to $155+ billion by 2019 (Cybersecurity Industry, http://cybersecurityventures.com/cybersecurity-market-report/).

Worldwide spending on information security was expected to reach $71.1 billion in 2014, with the data loss prevention segment recording the fastest growth at 18.9%, according to a forecast from Gartner, Inc. Total information security spending is expected to grow a further 8.2% in 2015 to reach $76.9 billion.

The Cyber Security Market 2015–2025: Leading Companies in Network, Data, Endpoint, Application & Cloud Security, Identity Management & Security Operations report by Visiongain indicates that the cybersecurity market is set to be worth $75.4 billion in 2015 (a small percentage difference compared to Gartner's estimate for 2015), as high-demand continues for information security solutions.

The cybersecurity market is estimated to grow to $155.74 billion by 2019, at a compound annual growth rate (CAGR) of 10.3% from 2014 to 2019, according to a report from Markets and Markets. The aerospace, defense, and intelligence vertical continues to be the largest contributor to cybersecurity solutions. North America is expected to be the biggest market, while the Asia Pacific (APAC) and Europe, the Middle East, and Africa (EMEA) regions are expected to experience increased market traction.

"Next generation" cybersecurity spending could reach $15 billion to $20 billion in the next 3 years.

FBR Capital Markets was quoted in a recent *CIO Journal* (published by *The Wall Street Journal*) article as predicting a 20% increase in "next-generation cybersecurity spending" in 2015, as companies move beyond traditional firewall and endpoint vendors to cloud and Big Data solutions.

Approximately 10% of enterprises and government agencies have upgraded to next-generation security software, such as firewalls that detect and block threats at the application level or Big Data analytics services geared toward security, said FBR Capital Markets managing director and senior research analyst Daniel Ives. "The market for those software tools could be $15 billion to $20 billion over the next three years" added Ives.

"Hackers and nation states are increasingly targeting websites in an attempt to gain illicit access to enterprise networks and highly valuable digital assets," said Frost & Sullivan network security senior industry analyst Chris Rodriguez (April 2015). "Since Web applications present a number of unique security challenges that require purpose-built security solutions, such high profile data breaches have piqued the demand for WAF (web application firewall) systems. The worldwide market is expected to reach $777.3 million in 2018."

Global spending on mobile and network security is estimated at $11 billion annually, and growing.

According to Gartner, nearly 2.2 billion smartphones and tablets were sold to end users in 2014. Gartner predicts that by 2017, nearly 75% of mobile security breaches will be the result of mobile application misconfiguration.

"In 2014 in the US, mobile web traffic exceeded desktop web traffic for the first time as mobile has become the most convenient and cost-effective way to get online" says Yuval Ben-Itzhak, Chief Technology Officer at AVG Technologies, one of the largest providers of consumer security, privacy, performance, and backup mobile applications and software for Windows, iOS, and Android devices. "So in 2015, we will see mobile apps becoming the primary target for hackers, with apps left unmaintained by developers in App Stores being among the most vulnerable" he says.

According to Ernst & Young's (EY) 2014 Global Information Security Survey, security teams' biggest increases in spending will revolve around mobile technology (46%), followed by cloud and virtualization (43%), data leakage (41%), and identity and access management (39%).

According to Infonetics Research, the mobile device security market is expected to grow to $3.4 billion in 2018.

The Mobile Security (mSecurity) Bible: 2014–2020—Device Security, Infrastructure Security & Security Services report published by SNS Research estimates that mobile device and network security investments accounted for nearly $11 billion in 2014 alone. The market is further expected to grow at a CAGR of nearly 20% over the next 6 years.

According to SNS Research, installation of antimalware/antivirus client software is fast becoming a de facto requirement for most smartphones and tablets. Furthermore, mobile device original equipment manufacturers are also integrating advanced biometrics such as fingerprint sensing into their smartphones and tablets, amid growing popularity of security sensitive opportunities such as mobile payments.

There's a tidal wave of opportunity for mobile security firms with the right strategies and offerings. One company riding the wave is SnoopWall, Inc., the world's first counterveillance software development company focused on mobile app security. "Mobile-device security will become the top requirement this year (2015) for mobile banks, retailers and wallets as they move all their transactions into our space," says Gary Miliefsky, SnoopWall's CEO. "That's why we developed our SDK, to provide protection for their apps against the hundreds of millions of pieces of undetectable malware disguised as free trustworthy apps—just waiting to steal valuable personally identifiable information in the blink of an eye." SnoopWall is listed at #90 on the Cybersecurity 500. Security will become the killer app for big data analytics.

The big data and analytics market will reach $125 billion worldwide in 2015, according to research firm IDC. Big data analytics tools will be the first line of defense, combining machine learning, text mining, and ontology modeling to provide holistic and integrated security threat prediction, detection, and deterrence and prevention programs, according to recent predictions by The International Institute of Analytics (IIA).

The Internet of Things (IoT) analytics will be hot, with a 5-year CAGR of 30%, according to IDC. IoT will be the next critical focus for data/analytics services, according to IDC. While the IoT trend has focused on the data generation and production (sensors) side of the equation, the "Analytics" of Things is a particular form of big data analytics that often involves anomaly detection and "bringing the data to the analytics" according to IIA.

"Cybersecurity Ventures is expecting the big data security analytics space to be very competitive with even more new entrants over the next year and a crowded field of vendors battling for market share" says Steve

Morgan, editor-in-chief of the *Cybersecurity Market Report*. "It is a converged space with established companies coming in from different sectors and viewpoints (big data, analytics, network monitoring, logging, etc.), plus pure-play VC funded startups" adds Morgan.

6.2 MANAGING RISK IN THE CLOUD

Because of economies of scale, cloud providers have the potential to offer state-of-the-art cloud ecosystems that are resilient and secure—far more secure than the environments of consumers who manage their own systems. This has the potential to greatly benefit many organizations. In Chapter 3, we discussed the need for businesses to gain visibility into a cloud provider's service, to build the necessary trust and properly weigh the benefits of adopting a cloud-based solution to store a cloud consumers' data. The sensitivity of the stored information needs to be considered against the incurred security and privacy risks. For example, the benefits of a cloud-based solution would depend on the cloud model, type of cloud service considered, the type of data involved, the system's criticality/impact level, the cost savings, the service type, and any associated regulatory requirements.

Cloud-based information systems are exposed to *threats* that can have adverse effects on organizational operations (i.e., missions, functions, image, or reputation), organizational assets, individuals, and other organizations. Malicious entities can exploit both known and unknown vulnerabilities to compromise the confidentiality, integrity, or availability of the information being processed, stored, or transmitted by those systems.

There are many types of risk that organizations need to address: program management, investment, budget, legal liability, safety, inventory, supply chain, security, and more. Risk management can be viewed as a holistic activity that is fully integrated into every aspect of the organization. Risk management activities can be grouped into three categories based on the level at which they address the risk-related concerns:

a. The *organization* level (tier 1)

b. The *mission and business process* level (tier 2)

c. The *information system* level (tier 3)

Risk management needs to be a cyclically executed process composed of a set of coordinated activities for overseeing and controlling risks. This process targets the enhancement of strategic and tactical security and includes the execution of a *risk assessment*, the implementation of a *risk mitigation* strategy, and the employment of *risk control* techniques and procedures for the continuous monitoring of the security state of the information system. Cloud-based information systems, as with traditional information systems, require that risks be managed throughout the system development life cycle (SDLC).

In this chapter, we focus only on the tier 3 security risk related to the operation and use of cloud-based *information systems*. To prevent and mitigate any threats, adverse actions, service disruptions, attacks, or compromises, organizations need to quantify their *residual risk* below the *threshold* of the acceptable level of risk.

The information systems risk management (tier 3 risk management) is guided by the risk decisions at tier 1 and tier 2. Risk decisions at tiers 1 and 2 affect the ultimate selection of the organization's systems on the basis of their data sensitivity, the suitable cloud architecture,* and the safeguards and countermeasures (i.e., security controls) at the information system level. Information security requirements are satisfied by the selection of appropriate management, operational, and technical security controls from standardized catalogs of security and controls (i.e., National Institute of Standards and Technology [NIST] Special Publication 800-53 Revision 4, ISO/IEC 27001, ISO/IEC 27002, etc.).

In a cloud ecosystem, the complex relationships among cloud actors, the actors' individual missions, business processes, and their supporting information systems require an integrated, ecosystem-wide risk management framework (RMF) that addresses all cloud actors' needs. As with any information system, for a cloud-based information system, cloud actors are responsible for evaluating their *acceptable risk*, which depends on the threshold set by their *risk tolerance* to the cloud ecosystem-wide *residual risk*.

To effectively manage information security risk at the ecosystem level, the following high-level elements must be established:

- Assignment of risk management responsibilities to the cloud actors involved in the orchestration of the cloud ecosystem. Internally, each cloud actor needs to further assign responsibilities to their senior leaders, executives, and representatives.

---

* Cloud architecture combines a cloud deployment type (public, private, hybrid, community) and cloud service model (Infrastructure as a Service [IaaS], Platform as a Service [PaaS], and Software as a Service [SaaS]).

FIGURE 6.1   Video lecture: cloud risks, threats, and mitigation strategies.

- Establishment of the cloud ecosystem-wide tolerance for risk and communicate this risk tolerance through their service level agreement (SLA), including the information on decision-making activities that affect the risk tolerance.

- Near real-time monitoring, recognition, and understanding, by each cloud actor, of the information security risks arising from the operation and use of the information system leveraging the cloud ecosystem.

- Accountability by the cloud actors and near real-time information sharing of the cloud actors' incidents, threats, risk management decisions, and solutions (Figure 6.1).

6.2.1 The Risk Management Framework

Risk is often expressed as a function of the *likelihood* that an adverse outcome occurs, multiplied by the *magnitude* of such an adverse outcome. In information security, *likelihood* is understood as a function of the threats to the system, the vulnerabilities that can be exploited, and the consequences of those vulnerabilities being exploited. Accordingly, security *risk assessments* focus on identifying where in the cloud ecosystem damaging events could take place.

The risk-based approach of managing information systems is a holistic activity that needs to be fully integrated into every aspect of the organization, from planning to SDLC processes, to security controls allocation and continuous monitoring. Therefore, an RMF provides a disciplined and structured process that integrates information security and risk management activities into the SDLC. An RMF operates primarily at tier 3 in the risk management hierarchy, but it can also have interactions at tier 1 and tier 2. Some example interactions include providing the risk executive with feedback from ongoing monitoring and from authorization decisions, disseminating the updated risk information to authorizing officials and to information system owners, and so on.

The RMF illustrated in Figure 6.2 reproduces the NIST Special Publication (SP) 800-37 Revision 1 risk management process—a process government agencies and private sector organizations have vetted as a best practice for their traditional information systems. As stated in NIST SP 800-37 Rev. 1, *Guide for Applying the Risk Management Framework to Federal Information Systems*, defining information system requirements is a critical part of any system development process and needs to begin in a system's initiation phase. Since the security requirements are a subset of the overall functional and nonfunctional requirements, security requirements need to be integrated into the SDLC simultaneously with the functional and nonfunctional requirements. The security requirements need to be defined, and solutions should be researched and engineered from inception of the system's development. Treating security as a patch or addition to the system and architecting and implementing solutions

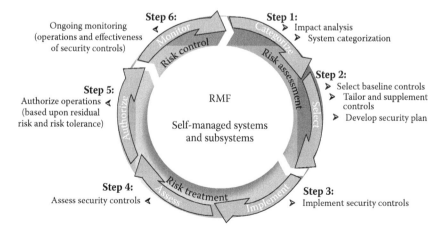

FIGURE 6.2   Risk management framework (NIST SP 800-37 Rev. 1).

independent of the SDLC is a more difficult process that can incur higher costs with a lower potential to effectively mitigate risk.

The process of applying the RMF's six well-defined, risk-related steps should be executed concurrently by selected individuals or groups in well-defined organizational roles, as part of (or in parallel with) the SDLC process. These steps or tasks are also listed in Table 6.1, in alignment with the risk management actions described earlier in this section.

NIST SP 800-37 Rev. 1 provides detailed information regarding security categorization, security control selection, security control implementation,

TABLE 6.1   Risk Management Activities and RMF Steps (NIST SP 800-37 Rev. 1)

Risk assessment (analyze cloud environment to identify potential vulnerabilities and shortcomings)	**Step 1: Categorize** the information system and the information processed, stored, and transmitted by that system based on a **system impact analysis**. Identify operational, performance, security, and privacy requirements.
	Step 2: Select, on the basis of the security categorization, the initial set of security controls for the information system (referred to as baseline security controls). Then, tailor and supplement the baseline security controls set on the basis of the organizational assessment of risk and the conditions of the operational environment. Develop a strategy for the continuous monitoring of security control effectiveness. Document all the controls in the security plan. Review and approve the security plan.
Risk treatment (design mitigation policies and plans)	**Step 3: Implement** the security controls and describe how the controls are employed within the information system and its environment of operation.
	Step 4: Assess the security controls using appropriate assessment procedures as documented in the assessment plan. The assessment determines if the controls are implemented correctly and if they are effective in producing the desired outcome.
	Step 5: Authorize information system operation on the basis of the determined risk resulting from the operation of the information system and the decision that this risk is acceptable. The assessment is performed considering the risk to organizational operations (including mission, functions, image, or reputation), organizational assets, individuals, and other organizations.
Risk control (risk monitoring— surveying, reviewing events, identifying policy adjustments)	**Step 6: Monitor** the security controls in the information system on an ongoing basis including assessing control effectiveness, documenting changes to the system or its environment of operation, conducting security impact analyses of these changes, and reporting the security state of the system to designated organizational officials.

security control assessment, information system authorization, and security control monitoring. The document promotes the concept of near real-time risk management and ongoing information system authorization through the implementation of robust continuous monitoring processes. The reader is encouraged to review NIST SP 800-37 Rev. 1, which is leveraged here for the current discussion of applying the RMF in a cloud ecosystem. It is important to note that although the NIST document addresses complex information systems composed of multiple subsystems operated by different entities, it does not address cloud-based information systems, or any other kind of systems that leverage utility-based resources.

When orchestrating a cloud ecosystem for a cloud-based information system, cloud consumers, as owners of the data associated with the system, remain responsible for securing the system and the data commensurate with the data sensitivity. However, the cloud consumers' level of control and direct management varies based on the cloud deployment model.

Figure 6.3 is building upon the consumer's level of control discussed in Chapter 3 and illustrates this aspect in parallel with the RMF applied to different layers of the functional stack, showing that for an IaaS cloud, the cloud consumer manages the top part of the functional stack above the hypervisor, while the consumer-managed functional stack proportionally decreases for a PaaS cloud and is reduced to a minimum in a SaaS cloud ecosystem.

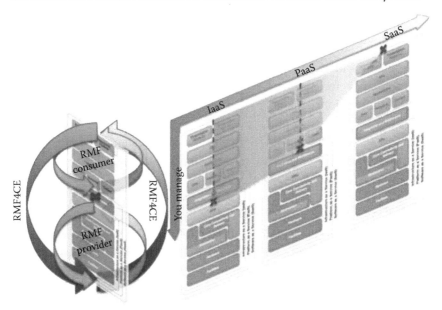

FIGURE 6.3   Applying RMF to a cloud ecosystem (RMF4CE).

As stated above, Figure 6.3 also shows that the RMF process listed in Table 6.1 and in NIST SP 800-37 Rev. 1 is applicable by a cloud actor to the layers of the functional stack that are under management. In a simplified cloud ecosystem model, which is orchestrated only by the cloud consumer and the cloud provider, the RMF as listed in Table 6.1 is applied by the cloud provider to the lower part of the stack, which is built as part of the service offered. Cloud consumers will apply the RMF to the upper functional layers, the ones built and deployed on top of the cloud infrastructure offered as a service.

However, before acquiring a cloud service, a cloud consumer needs to analyze the risk associated with the adoption of a cloud-based solution for a particular information system and plan for the risk treatment and risk control activities associated with the cloud-based operations of this system. To do so, a cloud consumer needs to gain the perspective of the entire cloud ecosystem that will serve the operations of their cloud-based information system. Cloud consumers must also apply the RMF in a customized way that allows them to

- Perform a risk assessment
- Identify the best-fitting cloud architecture
- Select the most suitable cloud service
- Gain necessary visibility into the cloud offering
- Define and negotiate necessary risk treatment and risk control mitigations before finalizing the SLA and proceeding with the security authorization

Figure 6.3 depicts this RMF for the cloud ecosystem (RMF4CE) from the cloud consumer's perspective, showing it as a repeatable process that encompasses the entire cloud ecosystem.

6.2.2 Cloud Providers Risk Management Process

Cloud providers develop cloud architectures and build cloud services that incorporate core functionality and operational features, including security and privacy controls that meet baseline requirements. Their solutions aim to satisfy the needs of a large pool of cloud consumers in a way that requires minimum customization. A cloud provider's selection and implementation of its security and privacy controls considers their effectiveness, efficiency, and constraints based on applicable laws, directives, policies, standards, or regulations with which the cloud provider must comply. The cloud consumers' specific requirements and mandates are not known and therefore are projected as a generic core set.

Figure 6.3 depicts the *service boundaries* for IaaS, PaaS, and SaaS, respectively, illustrating the set of resources allocated to a cloud service. Cloud providers have significant flexibility in determining what constitutes a cloud service and therefore its associated boundary, but at the time the system is architected and implemented, they can only assume the nature of data their cloud consumers will generate. Therefore, the security and privacy controls selected and implemented by a cloud provider are sets that meet the needs of a large number of potential consumers. However, the centralized nature of the offered cloud service enables a cloud provider to engineer highly technical, specialized security solutions that can provide a higher security posture than that in traditional IT systems.

Applying standardized or well-vetted approaches to cloud service risk management is critical to the success of the entire cloud ecosystem and its supported information systems. Since the offered cloud service is directly managed and controlled by the cloud provider, applying the RMF to this system does not require additional tasks beyond those of a classical IT system; therefore, the risk management approach described above is a good example of a broadly accepted, well-vetted approach.

It is important to note that the security posture of a cloud ecosystem is only as strong as the weakest subsystem or functional layer. Since a cloud provider's reputation and business continuity depend on the smooth operation and high performance of their consumers' solutions, when applying the RMF, a cloud provider aims to compensate for possible weakness in their cloud consumers' solutions.

6.2.3 Cloud Consumers Risk Management Process

Generally speaking, organizations are more comfortable accepting risk when they have greater control over the processes and equipment involved. A high degree of control enables organizations to weigh alternatives, set priorities, and act decisively in their own best interest when faced with an incident. For successful adoption of a cloud-based information system solution, the cloud consumer must be able to clearly understand the cloud-specific characteristics of the system, the architectural components for each service type and deployment model, and the cloud actors' roles in establishing a secure cloud ecosystem. Furthermore, it is essential to cloud consumers' business and mission-critical processes that they have the ability to (a) identify all cloud-specific, risk-adjusted security and privacy controls; (b) request from the cloud providers and brokers—when applicable and via contractual means—service agreements and SLAs where the implementation of security and privacy controls is the cloud providers' responsibility; (c) assess the implementation of said security and privacy controls; and (d) continuously monitor all identified security and privacy controls.

Since the cloud consumers are directly managing and controlling the functional capabilities they implement, applying the RMF to these functional layers does not require additional tasks or operations than necessary in a classical information technology (IT) system; therefore, the risk management approach described above is a good example of a broadly accepted, well-vetted approach.

With cloud-based services, some subsystems or subsystem components fall outside of the direct control of a cloud consumer's organization. Since the adoption of a cloud-based solution does not inherently provide for the same level of security and compliance with the mandates in the traditional IT model, being able to perform a comprehensive *risk assessment* is key to building trust in the cloud-based system as the first step in authorizing its operation. Characteristics of a cloud ecosystem include the following:

- Broad network access

- Decreased visibility and control by cloud consumers

- Dynamic system boundaries and comingled roles/responsibilities between the cloud consumer and cloud provider

- Multitenancy

- Data residency

- Measured service

- Significant increase in scale (on demand), dynamics (elasticity, cost optimization), and complexity (automation, virtualization)

These characteristics often present a cloud consumer with security risks that are different from those in traditional IT solutions. To preserve the security level of their information system and data in a cloud-based solution, cloud consumers need the ability to identify all cloud-specific, risk-adjusted security and privacy controls in advance. They must also request from the cloud providers and brokers, through contractual means and SLAs, that all security and privacy components are identified and that their controls are fully and accurately implemented.

Understanding the relationships and interdependencies between the different Cloud Computing deployment models and service models is critical to understanding the security risks involved in Cloud Computing. The differences in methods and responsibilities for securing different combinations of service and deployment models present a significant challenge for cloud consumers. They need to perform a thorough *risk assessment*, to accurately identify the security and privacy controls necessary to preserve the security level of their environment as part of the *risk treatment* process, and to monitor the operations and data after migrating to the cloud in response to their *risk control* needs.

Cloud consumers are currently facing several challenges when seeking to determine which cloud service offering most effectively addresses their Cloud Computing requirement(s) while supporting their business and mission-critical processes and services in the most secure and efficient manner. The objective of this section is to apply, from the cloud consumer's perspective, the RMF and to demystify for the cloud consumers the process of describing, identifying, categorizing, analyzing, and selecting cloud-based services.

In general, a cloud consumer adopting a cloud-based solution needs to follow these steps:

1. Describe the service or application for which a cloud-based solution may be leveraged.

2. Identify all functional capabilities that must be implemented for this service.

3. Identify the security and privacy requirements and the security controls needed to secure the service or application. For adopters of NIST standards and guidelines, cloud consumers need to determine the security category and associated impact level of information systems in accordance with Federal Information Processing Standard (FIPS) 199, *Standards for Security Categorization of Federal Information and Information Systems*, and FIPS 200, *Minimum Security Requirements for Federal Information and Information Systems*, respectively. The information system's impact level determines the security control baseline that needs to be implemented. Three sets of baseline controls correspond to low-impact, moderate-impact, and high-impact information systems.

4. Analyze and select the most appropriate cloud ecosystem architecture, by combining a cloud deployment model (public, private, hybrid, community) and cloud service model (IaaS, PaaS, SaaS):

- Public IaaS, Public PaaS, and Public SaaS

- Private IaaS, Private PaaS, and Private SaaS

- Hybrid IaaS, Hybrid PaaS, and Hybrid SaaS

- Community IaaS, Community PaaS, and Community SaaS

5. Identify and select the cloud actors involved in orchestrating the cloud ecosystem (e.g., provider[s] and broker[s]).

6. Understand the cloud provider(s)' and broker(s)' security posture and inherited security and privacy controls. Tailor the security and privacy controls to fulfill the security and privacy requirements for the particular use case or identify additional compensating security controls, when necessary.

7. Assign specific values to organization-defined security parameters via explicit assignment and selection statements.

8. Supplement baselines with additional security and privacy control enhancements, if needed.

9. Provide additional specification information for the implementation of security and privacy controls.

On the basis of the selected cloud ecosystem architecture, the organization would retain and take upon itself the implementation of the security controls identified for the cloud consumer, augmented with the supplemental set of controls specific to the consumer's use case.

In Figure 6.4, we illustrate the RMF as applied to a cloud ecosystem from the cloud consumer's perspective. The additional operations and steps a cloud consumer needs to perform are highlighted in blue.

The RMF applied to the cloud ecosystem from the consumer's perspective can be used to address the security risks associated with cloud-based information systems by incorporating the outcome into the terms and conditions of the contracts with external cloud providers and cloud brokers. Performance aspects of these terms and conditions are also incorporated into the SLA, which is an intrinsic part of the security authorization

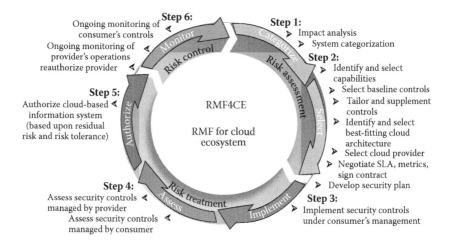

FIGURE 6.4   Cloud consumers' view of the RMF applied to a cloud ecosystem.

process and of SA between the cloud consumer, cloud provider, and broker (when applicable). Contractual terms should include guarantees of the cloud consumer's timely access to or provider's timely delivery of cloud audit logs, continuous monitoring logs, and any user access logs.

Table 6.2 aligns risk management activities with their corresponding steps from NIST SP 800-37 Rev. 1 and provides additional details that map to Figure 6.4.

The approach covered by the steps in Table 6.2 enables organizations to systematically identify their common, hybrid, and system-specific security controls and other security requirements to procurement officials, cloud providers, carriers, and brokers.

A cloud consumer remains responsible for performing a risk assessment, identifying all the security requirements for their cloud-based service(s), and selecting the appropriate security and privacy controls before selecting a cloud provider(s) and broker(s). Providers and brokers that best meet the cloud consumer's needs should be selected either directly or from a repository of authorized cloud suppliers. The cloud consumer needs to perform a thorough assessment, ideally using third-party independent assessors, to assess the risk from using this service. Successful creation of and migration to a robust cloud ecosystem depend on assessing a cloud provider's security posture and system performance, identifying remaining security and privacy controls that should be implemented to secure the service or application, and identifying the cloud actors responsible for implementing those controls. The set of remaining security and privacy

TABLE 6.2   RMF Applied to a Cloud Ecosystem—Cloud Consumer's Perspective

Risk Management Activities	NIST SP 800-37 RMF Steps	RMF Applied to a Cloud Ecosystem from the Cloud Consumer's Perspective
Risk assessment (analyze cloud environment to identify potential vulnerabilities and shortcomings)	1. Categorize	**Categorize** the information system and the information processed, stored, and transmitted by that system based on a **system impact analysis**. Identify operational, performance, security, and privacy requirements.
	2. Select (includes evaluate–select–negotiate)	Identify and **select** functional capabilities for the entire information system, the associated baseline security controls based on the system's impact level, the privacy controls, and the security control enhancements.
		Identify and **select** best-fitting cloud architecture for this information system.
		Evaluate/review cloud providers that meet consumer's criteria (architecture, functional capabilities, and controls).
		Select cloud provider(s) that best meet(s) the desired architecture and the security requirements (ideally should select the provider that provides as many controls as possible to minimize the number of controls that will have to be tailored).
		In the process, identify the controls that will be implemented by the consumer, the controls implemented by the provider as part of the offering, and the controls that need to be tailored (via compensating controls and parameter selection).
		Negotiate SLA, metrics, and sign SA as part of the procurement process.
		Document all the controls in the security plan. Review and approve the security plan.
Risk treatment (design mitigation policies and plans)	3. Implement	**Implement** security and privacy controls for which the cloud consumer is responsible.
	4. Assess	**Assess** the cloud provider's implementation of the tailored security and privacy controls.
		Assess the implementation of the security and privacy controls, and identify any inheritance and dependency relationships between the provider's controls and consumer's controls.
	5. Authorize	**Authorize** the cloud-based information system to operate.

(Continued)

TABLE 6.2 (CONTINUED)   RMF Applied to a Cloud Ecosystem—Cloud Consumer's Perspective

Risk Management Activities	NIST SP 800-37 RMF Steps	RMF Applied to a Cloud Ecosystem from the Cloud Consumer's Perspective
Risk control (risk monitoring— surveying, reviewing events, identifying policy adjustments)	6. Monitor	Continuous/near real-time **monitoring** of operations and effectiveness of the security and privacy controls under consumer's management.
		Continuous/near real-time **monitoring** of cloud provider's operations related to the cloud-based information system and assess the systems' security posture.
		Reassess and reauthorize (periodic or ongoing) the cloud provider's service.

controls needs to be addressed in agreements between the cloud consumer and other relevant cloud actors.

The SLA is the component of the SA that details the levels and types of services that are to be provided, including but not limited to the delivery time and performance parameters. Cloud providers use service-based agreements to describe their offerings and terms of service to potential cloud consumers. In some cases, a cloud consumer might be satisfied with the cloud provider's offer and service terms; however, there are instances when the cloud consumer is interested in a customer-based agreement and a customized service. The cloud consumer needs to pay special attention to the SLAs and involve the organizations' procurement, technical, and policy experts to ensure that the terms of the SLA will allow the organization to fulfill its mission and performance requirements.

A challenge in comparing and selecting service offerings is that cloud providers may offer a default contract written from the provider's perspective. Such default contracts may not adequately meet the cloud consumer's needs and may constrain the visibility of the cloud consumer into the delivery mechanisms of the service.

In summary, adopting a cloud-based solution for an information system requires cloud consumers to diligently identify their security requirement, assess each prospective service provider's security and privacy controls, negotiate SLA and SA, and build trust with the cloud provider before authorizing the service. A thorough risk analysis coupled with secure cloud ecosystem orchestration introduced in this book, along with adequate guidance on negotiating SLAs, are intended to assist the cloud consumer in managing risk and making informed decisions in adopting cloud services.

6.3 CYBERCRIME

6.3.1 The Hype

Cybercrime is on the rise and costing the world economy hundreds of billions of dollars annually. Companies across all industries worldwide have reported a total of 42.8 million detected attacks in 2014, according to the PWC Global State of Information Security Survey 2015. That is a 48% increase in incidents since the previous year.

Crime involving computers and networks has cost the world economy more than $445 billion annually, according to a 2014 report by the Center for Strategic and International Studies. The Justice Department (DOJ) has recently created a dedicated cybersecurity unit within its criminal division. "Given the growing complexity and volume of cyberattacks, as well as the intricate rubric of laws and investigatory tools needed to thwart the attacks, the cybersecurity unit will play an important role in this field," said Assistant Attorney General Leslie Caldwell during a speech at Georgetown University's law school. The new DOJ cyber team will "ensure that the powerful law enforcement tools are effectively used to bring the perpetrators (of crimes) to justice while also protecting the privacy of everyday Americans," added Caldwell.

Investigating cybercrimes—such as website hacks, intrusions, data theft, botnets, and denial of service attacks—is a top priority for the FBI. To keep pace with the evolving threat, the Bureau is appealing to experienced and certified cyber experts to consider joining the FBI to apply their well-honed tradecraft as cyber special agents. "The FBI seeks highly talented, technically trained individuals who are motivated by the FBI's mission to protect our nation and the American people from the rapidly evolving cyber threat," said Robert Anderson, Jr., executive assistant director for the Bureau's Criminal, Cyber, Response, and Services Branch. "What we want are people who are going to come and be part of a team that is working different, very complex types of investigations and to utilize their skillsets in that team environment" (source: fbi.gov).

Cybercrime is generating market opportunity for small cyber specialty companies—like fast-growing Autonomic Software in Danville, California, who is #40 on the Cybersecurity 500 list. "We are in the midst of tripling our revenues from year end 2014," says Tony Gigliotti, president at Autonomic Software. "We are currently working with one of the world's largest companies on unique ways to apply critical security updates to control process equipment, as well as U.S military allies for securing core I.T. applications. Our technology eliminates over 80% of all successful cyber attacks."

As cybercrime costs the world economy billions and helps create billions in revenue opportunity for vendors and service providers, cybercrime is also having a negative impact on companies seeking investment capital. According to new research from business consultancy KPMG, nearly 80% of investors would be put off investing in a business if it has been hacked or has an ineffective cybersecurity strategy. KPMG interviewed more than 130 global institutional investors responsible for more than $3 trillion of funds. "Investors are looking for cyber-resilient organizations as a means to gain comfort around the growing concern of their business and to protect their investment," said Matthew Martindale, director at KPMG.

6.3.2 The Facts

According to a 2015 Cybersecurity study by the Global Commission on Internet Governance,* when the normalized indicators of cybercrime are compared to the absolute numbers that are usually used to discuss the level of security in cyberspace, one of three misrepresentations occurs:

- The absolute numbers indicate that the situation is getting worse when the normalized numbers say it is getting better (as in the case of new vulnerabilities, zero-day vulnerabilities, browser vulnerabilities, mobile vulnerabilities, post-breach response costs, and notification costs).

- Both the absolute and the normalized numbers say the situation is worsening, but the absolute numbers say it is growing worse at a faster rate than the normalized numbers (as in the case of detection and escalation costs, when the full sample is considered).

- Both the absolute and the normalized numbers say the situation is improving, but the absolute numbers indicate a slower rate of improvement than the normalized numbers (as in the case of malicious web domains, botnets, web-based attacks since 2012, average per capita data breach costs, organizational costs attributed to data breaches, detection and escalation costs from 2010 to 2013, or lost business costs).

* https://www.cigionline.org/sites/default/files/no16_web_1.pdf.

In short, when the number of cyberattack vectors, the number of cyber-attacks, and the amount of damage caused by cybercrime are expressed as a proportion of the size of the Internet, each of the normalized numbers point to the idea that the security of cyberspace is better than is suggested by the unnormalized or absolute numbers. As a result, the security of cyberspace is likely better than is commonly perceived by the general public, private companies, and state officials.

This conceptualization of the security of cyberspace can be expressed as a function of three factors:

- The vectors available for cyberattack

- The occurrence of cyberattacks

- The damage caused by successful cyberattacks

Together, these three factors determine how secure cyberspace is for an individual user.

6.3.3 Cyberattack Vectors

Study data on cyberattack vectors led to the following conclusions:

- New vulnerabilities: new vulnerabilities normalized around the number of Internet users, a proxy for online devices in this case, fell from 3.56 new vulnerabilities per 1,000,000 Internet users in 2008 to 2.24 vulnerabilities per 1,000,000 Internet users in 2014. This drop amounts to a percentage change of 37.13%.

- Malicious web domains: the absolute number of new malicious domains has fallen from 55,389 malicious domains in 2008 to 29,927 malicious domains in 2014, a decline of 45.96%. The normalized numbers fell from 312.93 malicious domains per 1,000,000 domains in 2008 to only 103.91 malicious domains per 1,000,000 domains in 2014, which amounts to a decline of 66.79 percentage points.

- Zero-day vulnerabilities: the trend in zero-day vulnerabilities per 1,000,000 websites is declining over time, despite a jump upward in 2013.

- Browser vulnerabilities: the number of new browser vulnerabilities per 1,000,000,000 Google searches drops from 0.364 new vulnerabilities per 1,000,000,000 Google searches in 2008 to 0.305 new vulnerabilities per 1,000,000,000 Google searches in 2014, a decline of 16.23 percentage points.

- Mobile vulnerabilities: the number of new vulnerabilities per 1,000,000 gigabytes of mobile data fell from 0.29 vulnerabilities per 1,000,000 giga-bytes in 2009 to 0.0064 vulnerabilities per 1,000,000 gigabytes in 2014, a reduction of roughly 97.7 percentage points. Active mobile broadband subscriptions, for their part, fell from 0.273 new vulnerabilities per 1,000,000 subscriptions in 2009 to 0.086 vulnerabilities per 1,000,000 subscriptions in 2014, a reduction of 68.43 percentage points. Finally, the number of new vulnerabilities per 1,000,000 smartphones sold fell from 0.826 in 2009 to 0.173 in 2013, a reduction of 79.02 percentage points.

When it comes to the potential vectors of cyberattack, the security of cyberspace is far better than what is shown by just looking at the abso-lute numbers. In four of the five vectors of attack (new vulnerabilities, zero-day exploits, browser vulnerabilities, and mobile vulnerabilities), the absolute numbers say that the situation is getting worse over time, while the normalized numbers show the opposite: cyberspace is becoming more secure. In the remaining case (malicious domains), both the absolute and the normalized numbers indicate an improving situation, but the former shows cyberspace getting better at a slower rate than the latter.

6.3.4 Occurrence of Cyberattacks

For this metric, the study looked at the occurrence of cyberattacks in absolute terms compared to the normalized trend between 2008 and 2014. Absolute numbers point to a strong escalatory trend in cyberattacks, indi-cating a worse level of security in cyberspace between 2008 and 2014. In contrast, the number of web-based attacks per 1,000,000 Internet users has only increased from 15,159.8 in 2008 to 489,756.7 in 2014, which is an increase of 3130.63%. The normalized trends also all suggest that, while the cyberspace security situation is definitely worse than in 2008 and 2009, the trend in normalized cyberattacks has improved since 2010 in the case of attacks per 1,000,000 websites, and since 2012 in the case of attacks per 1,000,000 Internet and 1,000,000 e-mail users. The absolute numbers sug-gest that, at best, the situation started to improve only in 2014, although it is possible that the low number of web-based attacks in 2014 is a statistical fluke rather than the start of a real trend in the absolute numbers.

6.3.5 Cost of Successful Cyberattacks

In analyzing this facet of cybersecurity, the study looked at six economic injuries that can be caused by a cyber incident, namely:

- Average cost per breach
- Organizational cost of a breach
- Average detection and escalation costs
- Post-breach response cost
- Lost business cost
- Notification costs

In two of the six tests, post-breach response costs and notification costs, the absolute numbers point to a worsening situation, while the normalized numbers actually indicate that costs are declining. In three of the six cases (average cost per capita, overall organizational costs, and lost business costs), both sets of numbers point to an improving situation, but the normalized numbers show the situation improving faster than the absolute numbers. Finally, in the last case (detection and escalation costs), both sets of numbers say the situation is getting worse, but the absolute numbers say that things are falling apart faster than the normalized numbers.

Any conclusions drawn from this research need to be qualified in light of the relatively poor data that are available for study, but overall, these research results suggest that the security of cyberspace is actually better than what most may think from looking just at the absolute numbers. Since these signs of insecurity in cyberspace are not worsening too quickly in most cases, the rapidly growing size of cyberspace actually means that the overall security of cyberspace is generally improving over time. This also provides significant support to a conclusion that current cybersecurity policies are most likely being very effective in countering the cybersecurity challenge.

6.4 EDUCATION AND TRAINING

Fast-growing security awareness training market exceeds $1 billion globally. The importance of computer security awareness training is supported by numerous recent reports including IBM's 2014 Cyber Security Intelligence Index, which found that 95% of all security incidents involve human error. Gartner, Inc. research vice president Andrew Wells said the security awareness training market exceeds $1 billion in annual revenue (globally) and is growing approximately 13% per year.

According to Gartner, based in Stamford CT, employees' actions can detrimentally affect security and risk performance. Chief information security officers (CISOs) and employee communication leaders are increasingly turning to educational security awareness solutions to help improve organizational compliance, expand security knowledge, and change poor security behaviors.

In the 2014 US State of Cybercrime Survey—cosponsors included Carnegie Mellon University and the Secret Service—28% of cybersecurity incidents were blamed on current or former employees, contractors, and other trusted parties. Nearly a third of respondents said such incidents cost more or inflict more damage than outside attacks.

Gartner released its inaugural Magic Quadrant for Security Awareness Computer-Based Training Vendors in Q4 2014, a report that reviewed the largest security awareness training vendors, plus many up-and-comers. The vendors in the Gartner report account for around $650 million in annual revenue.

In response to growing demand for security awareness and other education, training, and certification, Cybersecurity Ventures has launched a Directory of Top Cybersecurity Education and Training Providers.

6.5 TRENDS

The Managed Security Services Provider (MSSP) market is continuing to grow as companies look to outsource cybersecurity. Infonetics Research says the managed security market will exceed $9 billion by 2017, in its "Cloud and CPE Managed Security Services" report. Frost & Sullivan researchers predict that the EMEA MSSP market will reach $5 billion by 2018. "Threat intelligence, research, detection and remediation services are likely to grow at a rate twice that of security asset monitoring and management, becoming a critical focus area that will distinguish market leaders from the rest," stated Network Security Industry Principal, Frank Dickson.

"North American Managed Security Services will reach $3.25 billion in market revenue by 2018. Security asset management and monitoring will continue to be the largest market segment. Nonetheless, market growth will be driven by the emerging threat intelligence, research, detection, and remediation services segment—the nexus for industry innovation,"

according to Frost & Sullivan network security research director Frank
Dickson (April 2015).

Market intelligence from ABI Research finds that the global managed
security services market will be worth $15.4 billion by the end of 2015, and
will reach $32.9 billion in 2020. (ABI Research's market sizing in this mar-
ket category is substantially larger than Infonetics's or Frost & Sullivan's
market sizing—which appear to have similar projections.)

By 2018, Gartner projects that more than half of organizations will
use security services firms that specialize in data protection, security risk
management, and security infrastructure management to enhance their
security postures. They say that in 2015, roughly 10% of overall IT security
enterprise product capabilities will be delivered in the cloud, as cloud-
based services or cloud-managed products. For small or midsize businesses, Gartner projects that 30% of security controls will be cloud based
in 2015.

6.6 GLOBAL

Asia-Pacific spending on critical infrastructure security is set to hit $22 bil-
lion by 2020. ABI Research says active campaigns in cyberespionage and
cyberwarfare plague nation states and private sector organizations in the
Asia-Pacific region. Digitally advanced industries and emerging knowledge economies are lucrative targets for hostile cyber threat actors, fueled
by political ideals or financial gain.

Spending on critical infrastructure security is set to hit $22 billion by
2020 in the Asia-Pacific region, according to ABI Research's Cybersecurity
Strategies for Critical Infrastructure Market Research.

"The market for cybersecurity services is highly varied. Domestic ven-
dors will feature highly in Northeast Asian markets such as Japan, South
Korea, and China. However, there is significant opportunity for for-
eign security vendors to penetrate in Southeast Asian markets, notably
Australia, New Zealand, Malaysia, Indonesia, Thailand, and India," says
Michela Menting, practice director for digital security at ABI Research.

The Cybersecurity 500 list of companies is at www.Cybersecurity500
.com (Figure 6.5). Twenty-two percent of the Cybersecurity 500 listed
companies (110 companies) had international (non-US) headquar-
ters, a substantial increase over the Q1 2015 list. Countries outside the
United States with companies listed are as follows: United Kingdom (20
companies); Israel (16); Canada (13); Germany (12); France (5); Ireland,
The Netherlands, Denmark (4 each); Finland, China, Australia, Brazil

FIGURE 6.5   The Cybersecurity 500—www.Cybersecurity500.com—Word Cloud.

(3 each); Italy, Greece, Spain, Switzerland, Sweden, Romania, South Korea; Argentina (2 each); and Russia, Slovakia, Japan, Hong Kong, India, South Africa, Czech Republic, Singapore, Portugal (1 each).

The Cybersecurity 500 listing ranks companies based on feedback from CISOs, execution ability, and market buzz. A red-hot company at #9 on the list is Veracode, headquartered in Burlington, Massachusetts, which provides a market leading cloud platform for web and mobile application security scanning.

More professional services firms show up on the Cybersecurity 500.

"Unprepared organizations, when notified of a breach by external entities such as the FBI, are increasingly employing professional security service providers to address security emergencies," according to Frost & Sullivan network security research director Frank Dickson (April 2015). "Evasive malware and security skills shortages are driving demand for professional security services. Professional Security Services in North America will reach $1.9 billion in market revenue by 2018."

"Cybersecurity Ventures expects pure-play cybersecurity firms to outshine generalized IT VARs and systems integrators (who are developing security competencies) when it comes to CISOs who are selecting partners to help protect their enterprises," says Steve Morgan, editor-in-chief of the *Cybersecurity Market Report.* "CISOs are seeking peers and subject matter experts with deep experience to advise them on coping with today's sophisticated cyber threats and attackers, and to help select the right cybersecurity technologies and solutions," adds Morgan.

CHAPTER 7

Cloud Computing Vulnerabilities

I N 2013, THE CLOUD SECURITY ALLIANCE (CSA) did a study of cloud security vulnerabilities across the industry. The study reviewed 11,491 news articles on Cloud Computing–related outages from 39 news sources between January 2008 and February 2012. During this period, the number of cloud vulnerability incidents more than doubled over a 4-year period, increasing from 33 in 2009 to 71 in 2011. A total of 172 unique Cloud Computing outage incidents were reported, of which 129 (75%) made the cause of the outage public. The investigation revealed that the top three threats were "Insecure Interfaces and APIs" (51 incidents; 29% of all threats), "Data Loss and Leakage" (43 incidents; 25%), and "Hardware Failure" (18 incidents; 10%).

The data collected were a "best effort" attempt, largely because of the lack of transparency on vulnerabilities in the Cloud Computing industry. The data may therefore be incomplete for the following reasons:

1. The online news archive sources may not cover all cloud providers, owing to a bias toward the more prominent ones.

2. Although search engines can quickly filter findings based on key-words, the sites accessed are often those with high online network traffic. Hence, the incidents reported may be skewed.

3. Since the news articles are from online archives, some incidents before July 2011 when reporting began may have been dropped.

4. It is not mandatory for cloud providers to report incidents.

5. This investigation did not reflect the real impact of cloud operations in terms of the total cloud downtime hours, the total number of cloud users, and the total number of cloud applications affected, as such data were not disclosed. These quantifiable parameters together can objectively assess the severity of a disruption.

Study results indicate that the top three cloud providers, Amazon, Google, and Microsoft, account for approximately 56% of all nontransparent incidents of cloud vulnerability. Beginning in 2010, cloud providers became more transparent with their reports of cloud vulnerability incidents.

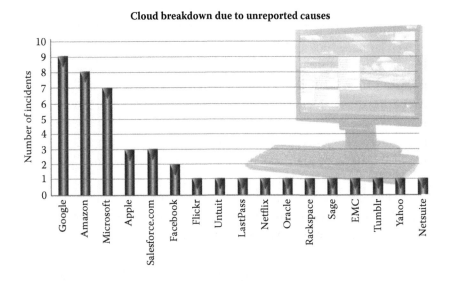

Cloud breakdown due to unreported causes

During the study time frame, the number of cloud vulnerability incidents rose with the number of cloud vulnerability incidents more than doubling from 2009 to 2011, most likely attributed to the explosive growth in cloud services. Threats were categorized as shown in Table 7.1 and the occurrence frequency was recorded by year (see the following figure).

TABLE 7.1   Cloud Threat Categories

Number	Category
1	Abuse and nefarious use of Cloud Computing
2	Insecure interfaces and APIs
3	Malicious insiders
4	Shared technology issues
5	Data loss or leakage
6	Account or service hijacking
7	Unknown risk profile
8	Hardware failure
9	Natural disasters
10	Closure of cloud service
11	Cloud-related malware
12	Inadequate infrastructure design and planning

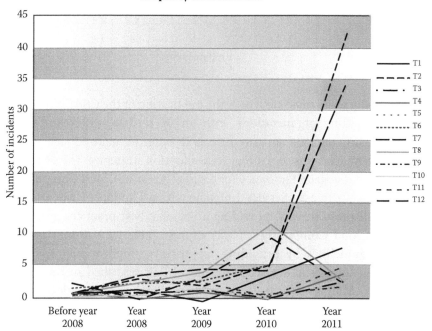

Frequency of cloud threats

A Pareto analysis reveals that Insecure Interfaces and APIs, Data Loss and Leakage, and Hardware Failure account for 64% of all cloud vulnerability incidents, although collectively they make up only 25% of total threats.

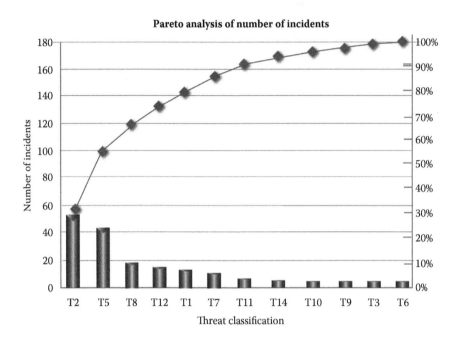

Pareto analysis of number of incidents

This study was a major drive for the publication of the CSA "Notorious Nine," providing organizations with an up-to-date, expert-informed understanding of cloud security threats in order to make educated risk-management decisions regarding cloud adoption strategies. The CSA also released the "Security Guidance for Critical Areas in Cloud Computing" and the "Security as a Service Implementation Guidance" when juxtaposed with these threats, providing a valuable best practices guide for securing Cloud Computing infrastructures. Table 7.2 summarizes the resultant guidelines by providing top threats, implications, and recommended infrastructure security controls, as described in the Cloud Controls Matrix (https://cloudsecurityalliance.org/download/cloud -controls-matrix-v3-0-1/).

TABLE 7.2   Recommended Security Controls for Top Cloud Computing Threats

Threat	Implication	Recommended Controls
Data breaches	Unfortunately, while data loss and data leakage are both serious threats to Cloud Computing, the measures you put in place to mitigate one of these threats can exacerbate the other. You may be able to encrypt your data to reduce the impact of a data breach, but if you lose your encryption key, you'll lose your data as well. Conversely, you may decide to keep offline backups of your data to reduce the impact of a catastrophic data loss, but this increases your exposure to data breaches.	CCM DG-04: Data Governance—Retention Policy CCM DG-05: Data Governance—Secure Disposal CCM DG-06: Data Governance—Non-Production Data CCM DG-07: Data Governance—Information Leakage CCM DG-08: Data Governance—Risk Assessments CCM IS-18: Information Security—Encryption CCM IS-19: Information Security—Encryption Key Management CCM SA-02: Security Architecture—User ID Credentials CCM SA-03: Security Architecture—Data Security/Integrity CCM SA-06: Security Architecture—Production/Non-Production Environments CCM SA-07: Security Architecture—Remote User Multi-Factor Authentication
Data loss	Under the new EU data protection rules, data destruction and corruption of personal data are considered forms of data breaches and would require appropriate notifications. Additionally, many compliance policies require organizations to retain audit records or other documentation. If an organization stores these data in the cloud, loss of that data could jeopardize the organization's compliance status.	CCM DG-04: Data Governance—Retention Policy CCM DG-08: Data Governance—Risk Assessments CCM RS-05: Resiliency—Environmental Risks CCM RS-06: Resiliency—Equipment Location

(Continued)

TABLE 7.2 (CONTINUED) Recommended Security Controls for Top Cloud Computing Threats

Threat	Implication	Recommended Controls
Account or service traffic hijacking	Account and service hijacking, usually with stolen credentials, remains a top threat. With stolen credentials, attackers can often access critical areas of deployed Cloud Computing services, allowing them to compromise the confidentiality, integrity, and availability of those services. Organizations should be aware of these techniques as well as common defense in depth protection strategies to contain the damage (and possible litigation) resulting from a breach. Organizations should look to prohibit the sharing of account credentials between users and services, and leverage strong two-factor authentication techniques where possible.	CCM IS-07: Information Security—User Access Policy CCM IS-08: Information Security—User Access Restriction/Authorization CCM IS-09: Information Security—User Access Revocation CCM IS-10: Information Security—User Access Reviews CCM IS-22: Information Security—Incident Management CCM SA-02: Security Architecture—User ID Credentials CCM SA-07: Security Architecture—Remote User Multi-Factor Authentication CCM SA-14: Security Architecture—Audit Logging/Intrusion Detection
Insecure interfaces and APIs	While most providers strive to ensure security is well integrated into their service models, it is critical for consumers of those services to understand the security implications associated with the usage, management, orchestration, and monitoring of cloud services. Reliance on a weak set of interfaces and APIs exposes organizations to a variety of security issues related to confidentiality, integrity, availability, and accountability.	CCM IS-08: Information Security—User Access Restriction/Authorization CCM SA-03: Security Architecture—Data Security/Integrity CCM SA-04: Security Architecture—Application Security

(Continued)

TABLE 7.2 (CONTINUED) Recommended Security Controls for Top Cloud Computing Threats

Threat	Implication	Recommended Controls
Denial of service	Experiencing a denial-of-service attack is like being caught in rush-hour traffic gridlock: there's no way to get to your destination, and nothing you can do about it except sit and wait. As a consumer, service outages not only frustrate you but also force you to reconsider whether moving your critical data to the cloud to reduce infrastructure costs was really worthwhile after all. Even worse, since cloud providers often bill clients based on the compute cycles and disk space they consume, there's the possibility that an attacker may not be able to completely knock your service off of the net, but may still cause it to consume so much processing time that it becomes too expensive for you to run and you'll be forced to take it down yourself.	CCM IS-04: Information Security—Baseline Requirements CCM OP-03: Operations Management—Capacity/Resource Planning CCM RS-07: Resiliency—Equipment Power Failures CCM SA-04: Security Architecture—Application Security

(Continued)

TABLE 7.2 (CONTINUED)   Recommended Security Controls for Top Cloud Computing Threats

Threat	Implication	Recommended Controls
Malicious insiders	A malicious insider, such as a system administrator, in an improperly designed cloud scenario can have access to potentially sensitive information. From IaaS to PaaS and SaaS, the malicious insider has increasing levels of access to more critical systems, and eventually to data. Systems that depend solely on the cloud service provider (CSP) for security are at great risk here. Even if encryption is implemented, if the keys are not kept with the customer and are only available at data-usage time, the system is still vulnerable to malicious insider attack.	CCM CO-03: Compliance—Third-Party Audits CCM DG-01: Data Governance—Ownership/Stewardship CCM DG-03: Data Governance—Handling/Labeling/Security Policy CCM DG-07: Data Governance—Information Leakage CCM FS-02: Facility Security—User Access CCM FS-05: Facility Security—Unauthorized Persons Entry CCM FS-06: Facility Security—Off-Site Authorization CCM HR-01: Human Resources Security—Background Screening CCM IS-06: Information Security—Policy Enforcement CCM IS-08: Information Security—User Access Restriction/Authorization CCM IS-10: Information Security—User Access Reviews CCM IS-13: Information Security—Roles/Responsibilities CCM IS-15: Information Security—Segregation of Duties CCM IS-18: Information Security—Encryption CCM IS-19: Information Security—Encryption Key Management CCM IS-29: Information Security—Audit Tools Access CCM RI-02: Risk Management—Assessments CCM SA-09: Security Architecture—Segmentation
Abuse of cloud services	This threat is more of an issue for cloud service providers than cloud consumers, but it does raise a number of serious implications for those providers. How will you detect people abusing your service? How will you define abuse? How will you prevent them from doing it again?	CCM IS-24: Information Security—Incident Response Legal Preparation CCM IS-26: Information Security—Acceptable Use

(Continued)

TABLE 7.2 (CONTINUED) Recommended Security Controls for Top Cloud Computing Threats

Threat	Implication	Recommended Controls
Insufficient due diligence	An organization that rushes to adopt cloud technologies subjects itself to a number of issues. Contractual issues arise over obligations on liability, response, or transparency by creating mismatched expectations between the CSP and the customer. Pushing applications that are dependent on "internal" network-level security controls to the cloud is dangerous when those controls disappear or do not match the customer's expectation. Unknown operational and architectural issues arise when designers and architects unfamiliar with cloud technologies are designing applications being pushed to the cloud. The bottom line for enterprises and organizations moving to a cloud technology model is that they must have capable resources, and perform extensive internal and CSP due diligence to understand the risks it assumes by adopting this new technology model.	CCM DG-08: Data Governance—Risk Assessments CCM IS-04: Information Security—Baseline Requirements CCM IS-12: Information Security—Industry Knowledge/Benchmarking CCM OP-03: Operations Management—Capacity/Resource Planning CCM RI-01: Risk Management—Program CCM RI-02: Risk Management—Assessments CCM RS-01: Resiliency—Management Program CCM RS-02: Resiliency—Impact Analysis CCM RS-03: Resiliency—Business Continuity Planning CCM SA-03: Security Architecture—Data Security/Integrity CCM SA-04: Security Architecture—Application Security

(Continued)

TABLE 7.2 (CONTINUED) Recommended Security Controls for Top Cloud Computing Threats

Threat	Implication	Recommended Controls
Shared technology vulnerabilities	A compromise of an integral piece of shared technology such as the hypervisor, a shared platform component, or an application in a SaaS environment exposes more than just the compromised customer; rather, it exposes the entire environment to a potential of compromise and breach. This vulnerability is dangerous because it potentially can affect an entire cloud at once.	CCM DG-03: Data Governance—Handling/Labeling/Security Policy CCM IS-04: Information Security—Baseline Requirements CCM IS-07: Information Security—User Access Policy CCM IS-15: Information Security—Segregation of Duties CCM IS-18: Information Security—Encryption CCM IS-20: Information Security—Vulnerability/Patch Management CCM SA-02: Security Architecture—User ID Credentials CCM SA-09: Security Architecture—Segmentation CCM SA-11: Security Architecture—Shared Networks CCM SA-14: Security Architecture—Audit Logging/Intrusion Detection

7.1 ORGANIZATIONAL REPORTING

7.1.1 IT/Cybersecurity Executive Title

Thirty-three percent of survey respondents reported that "CISO," "ISSO," or "CSO" was in their title. Other reported tiles include the following:

- "Director"—21%

- Specialist/Advisor/Consultant/Analyst/Administrator—10%

- CEO/President/Owner/XO/SVP—9%

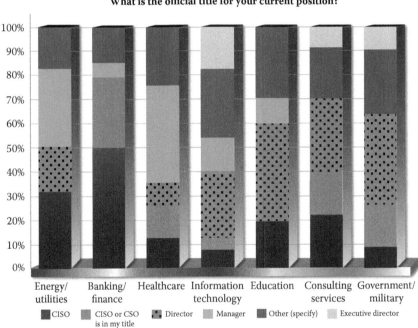

What is the official title for your current position?

7.2 ORGANIZATIONAL BUDGET MANAGEMENT

The importance of any business function is normally reflected in the assigned budget level. With this in mind, the CISO survey looked at budget level and control. Although most respondents reported the existence of a cybersecurity operational budget, the high percentage of organizations that reported to not have a budget, 43%, was surprising. Management of the cybersecurity budget seems to be driven mostly by industry norms and culture instead of by functional role.

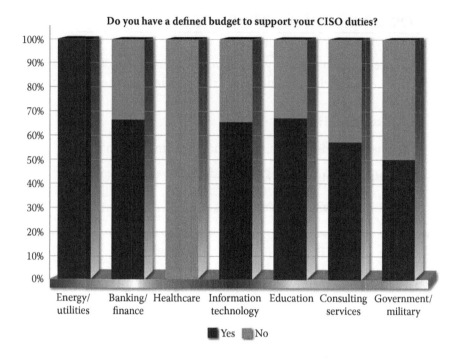

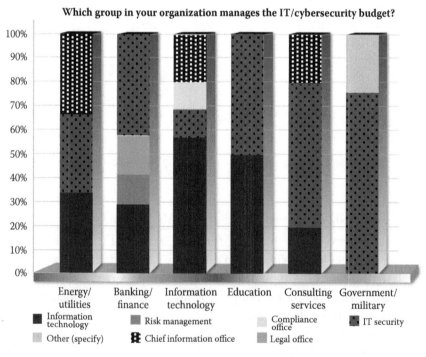

7.3 OPERATIONAL PLANNING

7.3.1 Key Required Resources

- Support of CIO/other organizational leaders—92%

- Adequate authority/enforcement ability—58%

- Adequate staffing/personnel—45%

- Adequate funding—43%

- Effective IT governance structure—33%

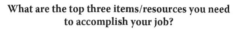

What are the top three items/resources you need to accomplish your job?

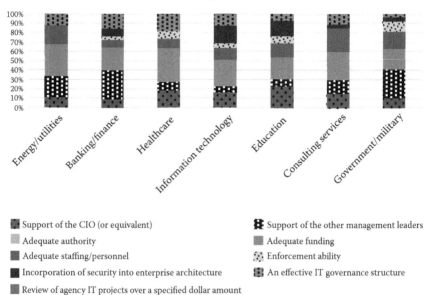

■ Support of the CIO (or equivalent)

□ Adequate authority

■ Adequate staffing/personnel

■ Incorporation of security into enterprise architecture

■ Review of agency IT projects over a specified dollar amount

■ Support of the other management leaders

■ Adequate funding

∴ Enforcement ability

■ An effective IT governance structure

7.3.2 Key Future Initiatives

- Incident response/management/breech notification

- Security awareness training

- Monitoring and threat awareness

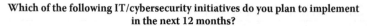

Which of the following IT/cybersecurity initiatives do you plan to implement in the next 12 months?

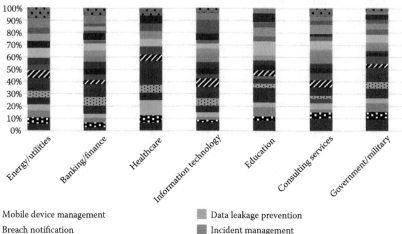

Mobile device management

Breach notification

Other (specify)

Security testing of applications (dynamic analysis, runtime observation)

Security assurance for software developed by third parties (outsourcing)

Security assurance for cloud-based (SaaS, IaaS, PaaS) services purchased by your organization

Security awareness and training for developers

Privacy

Continuous monitoring

Monitoring and threat awareness

Hardware purchase (e.g., firewalls, routers, intrusion detection systems)

Security awareness training

Data leakage prevention

Incident management

Threat and vulnerability management (e.g., security analytics, threat intelligence)

Security metrics and reporting

Security assurance for commercial off-the-shelf (COTS) purchases by your organization

Software development life cycle (SDLC) processes (e.g., secure coding, QA process)

Recruiting and retaining qualified application security resources

Penetration testing

Incident response

Software purchase (e.g., scanning tools, antivirus, data loss prevention applications)

Third-party risk assessment

7.3.3 Quality of Network IT/Cybersecurity

- Not existent—3%

- Somewhat satisfied—20%

- Mostly satisfied—41%

- Satisfied—25%

- Very satisfied—10%

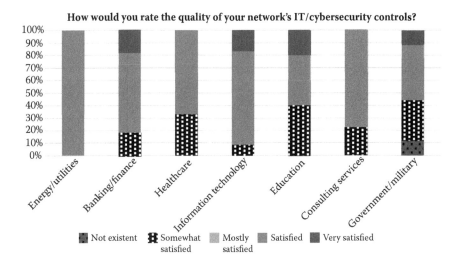

How would you rate the quality of your network's IT/cybersecurity controls?

Legend: ■ Not existent ■ Somewhat satisfied ■ Mostly satisfied ■ Satisfied ■ Very satisfied

7.3.4 Number of Security Breaches Experienced in the Past 2 Years

- None—45%

- One—25%

- Two—3%

- More than two—15%

- Not sure—12%

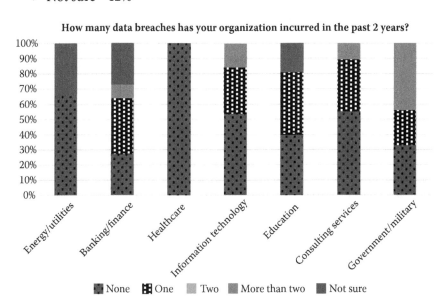

How many data breaches has your organization incurred in the past 2 years?

Legend: ■ None ■ One ■ Two ■ More than two ■ Not sure

7.3.5 Most Recent IT/Cybersecurity Risk Assessment

- Less than a year ago—67%

- Within the previous 2–5 years—18%

- More than 5 years ago—5%

- Never—10%

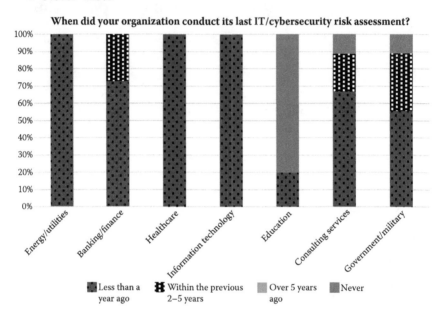

When did your organization conduct its last IT/cybersecurity risk assessment?

7.3.6 Source for Comparative IT/Cybersecurity Metrics

- Information Technology—57%

- Banking/Finance—31%

- Professional Services—22%

- Government/Military—20%

- Healthcare—19%

- Telecommunications—16%

- Energy/Utilities—12%

- Transportation—10%

- Consulting—10%

- Food and Agriculture—5%

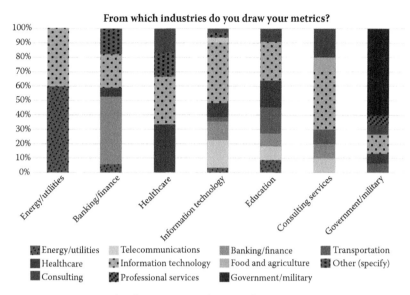

From which industries do you draw your metrics?

Energy/utilities · Telecommunications · Banking/finance · Transportation
Healthcare · Information technology · Food and agriculture · Other (specify)
Consulting · Professional services · Government/military

7.3.7 Security Standards/Frameworks Used

- NIST/FISMA—61%

- ITIL—45%

- ISO/IEC 27001:2005 27002:2005—43%

- PCI DSS—31%

Which of the following security standards or frameworks does your organization use?

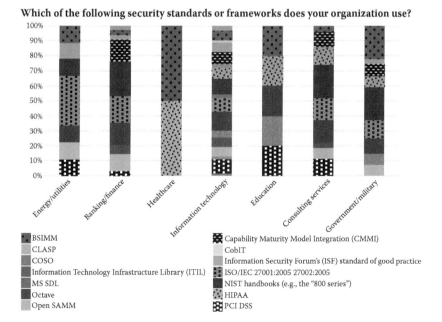

BSIMM · Capability Maturity Model Integration (CMMI)
CLASP · CobIT
COSO · Information Security Forum's (ISF) standard of good practice
Information Technology Infrastructure Library (ITIL) · ISO/IEC 27001:2005 27002:2005
MS SDL · NIST handbooks (e.g., the "800 series")
Octave · HIPAA
Open SAMM · PCI DSS

7.3.8 New Technology Strategy Posture

- We need to modify our strategy to address the new risks—51%

- Our current application security strategy adequately addresses the risks—25%

- We need to investigate further to understand the risks—22%

- We do not see any new or increased risks associated with these technologies—2%

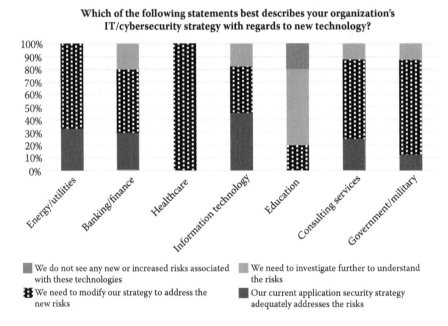

Which of the following statements best describes your organization's IT/cybersecurity strategy with regards to new technology?

- We do not see any new or increased risks associated with these technologies
- We need to investigate further to understand the risks
- We need to modify our strategy to address the new risks
- Our current application security strategy adequately addresses the risks

7.3.9 Cybersecurity Staffing Source

- Dedicated IT security staff—65%

- Partially consultant staffing—40%

- Additional duty for current employees—33%

- Outsourced completely—14%

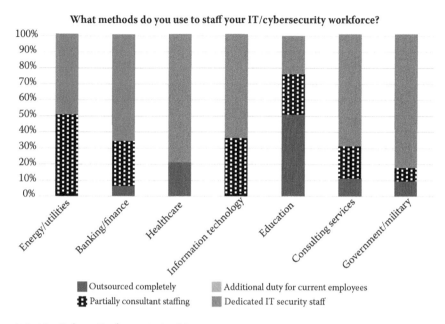

What methods do you use to staff your IT/cybersecurity workforce?

■ Outsourced completely
▦ Partially consultant staffing
□ Additional duty for current employees
▨ Dedicated IT security staff

7.3.10 Cyber Defense Priorities

- Cyber/Information security risk management—75%
- Compliance with regulatory requirements—63%
- Incident response capabilities—46%
- Infrastructure security—46%

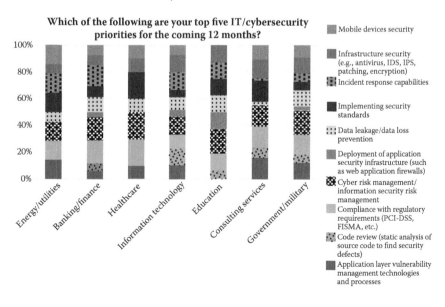

Which of the following are your top five IT/cybersecurity priorities for the coming 12 months?

- Mobile devices security
- Infrastructure security (e.g., antivirus, IDS, IPS, patching, encryption)
- Incident response capabilities
- Implementing security standards
- Data leakage/data loss prevention
- Deployment of application security infrastructure (such as web application firewalls)
- Cyber risk management/ information security risk management
- Compliance with regulatory requirements (PCI-DSS, FISMA, etc.)
- Code review (static analysis of source code to find security defects)
- Application layer vulnerability management technologies and processes

7.4 THREAT EXPECTATIONS

7.4.1 Type of Attack

- Targeted attacks—43%

- Malware—17%

- Illegitimate access—13%

- Account hijacking—11%

- DNS hijacking—6%

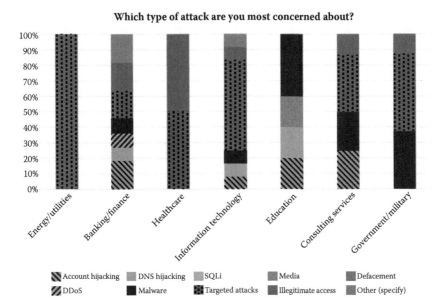

Which type of attack are you most concerned about?

7.4.2 Type of Attackers

- Criminal groups/professional fraudsters—64%

- Activists/anonymous—47%

- State-sponsored spies—43%

- Those involved in corporate/industrial espionage—38%

- Hobbyist hackers/insiders/employees—32%

- Competitors—15%

- Suppliers/partners—2%

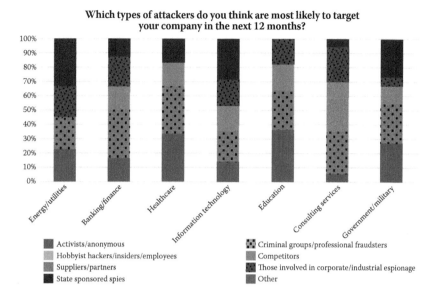

Which types of attackers do you think are most likely to target your company in the next 12 months?

Legend:
- Activists/anonymous
- Hobbyist hackers/insiders/employees
- Suppliers/partners
- State sponsored spies
- Criminal groups/professional fraudsters
- Competitors
- Those involved in corporate/industrial espionage
- Other

7.4.3 Application Security Risks

It is critical to understand that software language choice can have a big effect on application security. While some languages and programming models completely eliminate some security issues, an organization's choice is often driven more by other concerns such as the availability of skilled developers and the programming languages used by its suppliers. A recent study of vulnerabilities by industry shows that there are important differences across industries regarding the riskiness of their software.

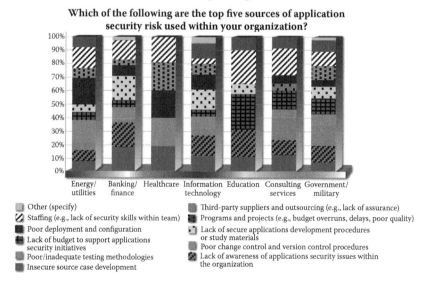

Which of the following are the top five sources of application security risk used within your organization?

Legend:
- Other (specify)
- Staffing (e.g., lack of security skills within team)
- Poor deployment and configuration
- Lack of budget to support applications security initiatives
- Poor/inadequate testing methodologies
- Insecure source case development
- Third-party suppliers and outsourcing (e.g., lack of assurance)
- Programs and projects (e.g., budget overruns, delays, poor quality)
- Lack of secure applications development procedures or study materials
- Poor change control and version control procedures
- Lack of awareness of applications security issues within the organization

One of the most important risks is the lack of awareness of application security issues within the organization. Software development teams themselves represent the greatest threat through the use of insecure source code development and lack of secure application development procedures.

Top 10 vulnerability categories by industry vertical

Vulnerability	Financial services	Government	Healthcare	Manufacturing	Retail and hospitality	Technology	Other	Rank
Code quality	65%	70%	80%	56%	68%	70%	65%	1
Cryptographics issues	60%	66%	61%	51%	63%	62%	59%	2
Information leakage	58%	62%	60%	49%	55%	62%	53%	3
CRLF injection	52%	52%	48%	45%	54%	54%	48%	4
Cross-site scripting (XSS)	49%	51%	46%	45%	52%	49%	47%	5
Directory traversal	48%	48%	45%	40%	44%	48%	46%	6
Insufficient input validation	41%	45%	43%	33%	44%	37%	37%	7
SQL injection	29%	40%	32%	31%	25%	30%	34%	8
Credential management	25%	40%	26%	24%	24%	28%	32%	9
Time and state	23%	19%	23%	17%	21%	26%	23%	10

Financial services have a much higher proportional use of Java and .NET and lower use of other languages. Manufacturing had the highest use of C++, followed by retail and hospitality and technology.

Healthcare and government consumed a disproportionately high share of .NET applications and manufacturing had the highest use of ColdFusion and Active Server Pages.

The use of mobile application also has a significant effect on an industry's security posture. In this area, technology and healthcare industry verticals are assessed with having a proportionally higher share of mobile applications. iOS use and Android use were roughly even in most industries, though iOS was slightly higher in healthcare.

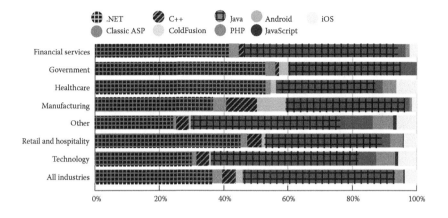

	.NET	Classic ASP	C++	ColdFusion	Java	PHP	Android	JavaScript	iOS
Financial services	42%	3%	2%	<1%	48%	2%	1%	<1%	2%
Government	52%	3%	1%	3%	35%	4%	0%	0%	0%
Healthcare	53%	2%	0%	2%	31%	3%	4%	0%	7%
Manufacturing	36%	4%	10%	9%	37%	1%	<1%	1%	2%
Other	24%	1%	4%	1%	47%	10%	7%	1%	7%
Retail and hospitality	45%	2%	5%	1%	37%	2%	4%	<1%	4%
Technology	30%	1%	4%	1%	46%	6%	6%	1%	6%
All industries	37%	3%	4%	2%	44%	4%	3%	<1%	4%

7.5 CYBERSECURITY OPERATIONS

7.5.1 Number of Security Positions

- Zero—5%

- 1–10—62%

- 11–30—9%

- 30–100—10%

- >100—9%

- Outsourced/don't know—5%

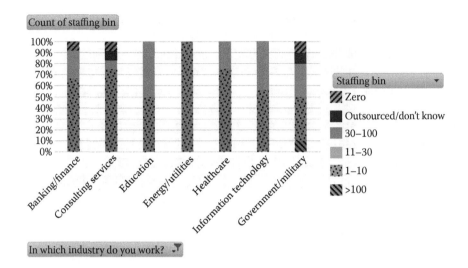

7.5.2 Key CISO Activities

- Policy and strategy—32%

- Day-to-day management—20%

- Coordinating and consulting—20%

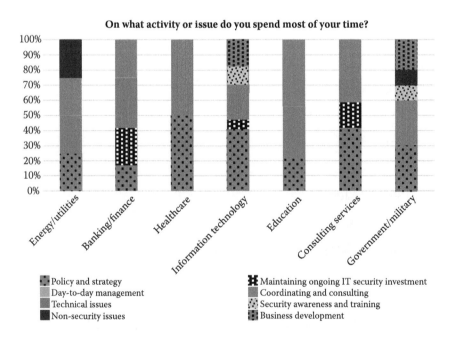

How are industries using the cloud? Figures 7.1 through 7.3 provide answers to this questions.

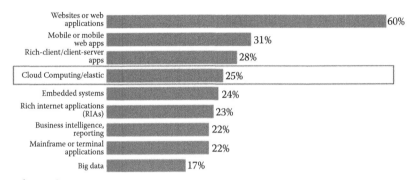

Base: Sample size = 1716.
Source: Forrester Business Technographics Global Developer Survey, 2014.

FIGURE 7.1   Which of the following types of development technologies have you worked with in the past 24 months? (Select all that apply.)

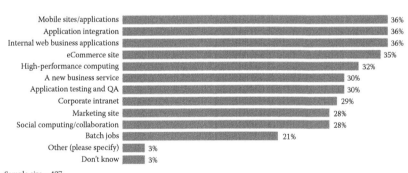

Base: Sample size = 427.
Source: Forrester Business Technographics Global Developer Survey, 2014.

FIGURE 7.2   Which of the following types of applications are you currently developing using cloud environment or have you delivered in a cloud environment in the past 12 months? (Select all that apply.)

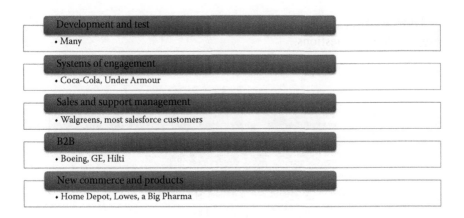

FIGURE 7.3   5 major adoption paths.

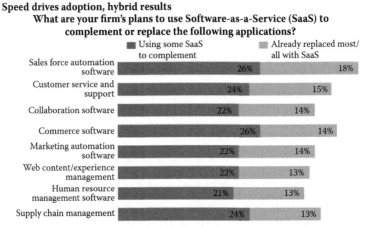

Change your sourcing

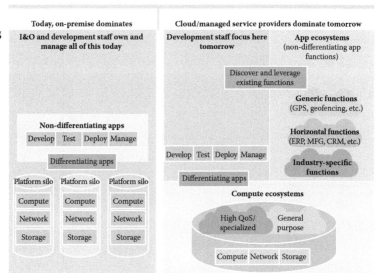

CHAPTER 8

General Cybersecurity Threat by Industry

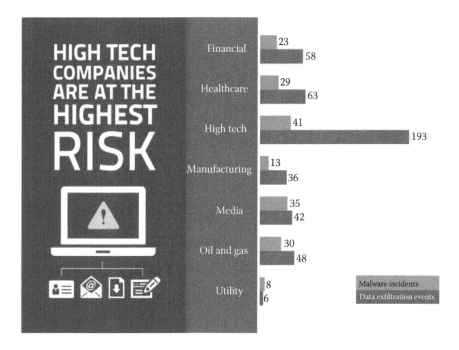

High-tech companies have the greatest cloud risk, averaging 193 data exfiltration events and 41 malware incidents per quarter. Companies in this category tend to have more permissive policies regarding the use of cloud services, which puts them at greater risk. The study found that despite having some of the most stringent data protection requirements, financial services and healthcare companies have a higher number of high-risk activities than other industries. Financial services had an average of 23 malware incidents per quarter and healthcare had 29 (http://info.skyhighnetworks.com/rs/skyhighnetworks/images/Skyhigh CloudAdoption%26RiskReport-Q22014.pdf).

In general, there are seven ways to move to the cloud (http://blogs.cisco .com/datacenter/seven-ways-to-move-to-the-cloud)

7 ways to move to the cloud

Move to the cloud

- Move to a new network cloud service, which has lower cost and higher bandwidth.

- Move to a new data center cloud service and move into a room that has colder air and bigger guard dogs.

- Move your application to a new compute and storage cloud service and let someone else manage the security, availability, and performance of the compute and storage.

- Move to a new software development cloud service and build the application you are thinking of moving. This might sound unreasonable, but with new tools, this is more possible than ever.

- Use a new operations management cloud service to manage the existing applications, meaning to manage the security, performance, and availability of that application.

- Have the vendor manage the application they sold you. In other words, the ISV that first sold you its on-premises application could now deliver that application as a service delivered and managed by the ISV.

- Finally, replace that application with a new generation of what I'll call a "born in the cloud" application cloud service.

Companies take their entire portfolio of applications and decide which of the seven they would implement. Companies should merge the answers into one plan so you can move from a strategic intent to a tactical plan (Interview, Timothy Chou).

This attack scenario was developed for the energy industry but is applicable to all:

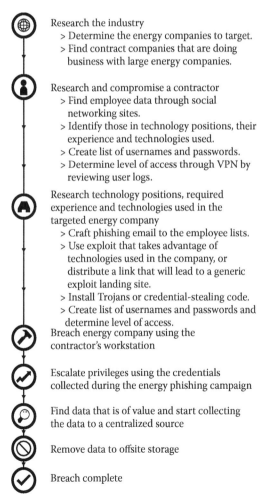

Research the industry
> Determine the energy companies to target.
> Find contract companies that are doing business with large energy companies.

Research and compromise a contractor
> Find employee data through social networking sites.
> Identify those in technology positions, their experience and technologies used.
> Create list of usernames and passwords.
> Determine level of access through VPN by reviewing user logs.

Research technology positions, required experience and technologies used in the targeted energy company
> Craft phishing email to the employee lists.
> Use exploit that takes advantage of technologies used in the company, or distribute a link that will lead to a generic exploit landing site.
> Install Trojans or credential-stealing code.
> Create list of usernames and passwords and determine level of access.

Breach energy company using the contractor's workstation

Escalate privileges using the credentials collected during the energy phishing campaign

Find data that is of value and start collecting the data to a centralized source

Remove data to offsite storage

Breach complete

(General description paragraphs from http://www.vormetric.com/data -security-solutions/industries).

8.1 ENERGY/UTILITIES

8.1.1 Vertical View (AlertLogic_Energy Sector_Cloud Security Report.pdf)

Companies in the energy sector are highly attractive targets for cyber-attacks. The Department of Homeland Security's (DHS') Industrial Control System-Cyber Emergency Response Team (ICS-CERT) found that, of the malware attacks reported to them in 2012, 41% were made on the systems of energy companies, such as grid operators and natural gas pipeline companies. Although the overall number of incidents reported was relatively small—198—the proportion aimed at energy was not. The sector receiving the next highest number of threats (Internet-facing industrial systems) experienced only 11% of them.

In an analysis of security incidents among its energy industry customers, Alert Logic found that energy companies are subjected to a broad range of attacks. Data captured over the period from April 1 to September 30, 2012, showed that 67% of Alert Logic's customers in the energy industry experienced brute force attacks (hackers looking for opportunistic points of vulnerability), while 61% were subject to malware/botnet attacks.

8.1.2 Energy-Specific Vulnerabilities

Supervisory Control and Data Acquisition (SCADA) systems are widely used in all critical infrastructure industries, including oil and gas pipelines and the electric grid, yet they are considered vulnerable to hacking.

Prevalence of subcontracting major energy sector companies (resource extraction) rely extensively on using smaller firms with limited information technology (IT) resources used as subcontractors. Their systems may be interconnected with those of the larger companies that hire them, making those larger companies more vulnerable to attacks. The costs associated with securing IT infrastructure have sometimes been weighed and found wanting when placed against the costs of doing nothing. Fixing the damage (or paying the fine) can sometimes be seen as the financially optimal choice.

The Bring Your Own Device (BYOD) trend can put corporate systems at significant risk. Even a seemingly harmless device like a USB thumb drive can be a virus carrier introducing catastrophic harm.

Whether or not they are bringing their own devices, employees are increasingly using their own applications (Bring Your Own Application [BYOA]) for collaboration, communication/social media, file transfer, and productivity.

As with BYOD and BYOA, there is nothing industry specific about the use of "worst practices" (e.g., password = 1234, employees accessing suspect sites while at work, etc.) in the energy sector. Still, in isolated locations (remote sites, oil rigs), introducing infected files by downloading music and video files occurs with some regularity.

Incident Class	Number of Incidents	Proportion of Incidents
Application attack	294	3.3%
Brute force	2699	30.5%
Denial of service	21	0.2%
Malware/botnet	4321	48.9%
Policy violation	117	1.3%
Reconnaissance-vulnerability scan	1123	12.7%
Web application attack	265	3.0%
Total	8840	

Incident Class	Percentage of Energy Sector Customers Impacted
Application attack	20.9%
Botnet/malware	76.7%
Brute force	60.5%
Denial of service	9.3%
Reconnaissance	23.3%
Vulnerability scar	34.9%
Web application attack	23.3%

Incident Class	Specific Incident Type	Percentage of Overall Incidents
Malware/botnet	Trojan activity	22.73%
Malware/botnet	Blackhole exploit kit download detected	11.01%
Brute force	Brute force (nonspecific)	9.73%
Brute force	Multiple failed SMB login attempts	6.76%
Brute force	RDP attempted administrator brute force attack	6.61%
Reconnaissance	Suspicious activity	5.88%
Brute force	SSH brute force attempt	4.42%
Malware/botnet	Blackhole exploit kit download attempt detected	3.35%
Web application attack	SQL injection exploit attempts	2.92%
Application attack	Application attack	2.83%

8.2 BANKING/FINANCE

8.2.1 Vertical View

Big banks and financial services firms ramp up cybersecurity spending in response to cyberattacks. According to the Banking & Financial Services Cybersecurity: U.S. Market 2015–2020 report, published by Homeland Security Research Corp. (HSRC), the 2015 US financial services cybersecurity market will reach $9.5 billion, making it the largest nongovernment cybersecurity market. In addition, the report concludes that this market will be the fastest-growing nongovernment cybersecurity market, exceeding $77 billion in cumulative 2015–2020 revenues.

JPMorgan Chase & Co. will likely double its $250 million annual security budget within 5 years, stated CEO Jamie Dimon in late 2014. JPMorgan disclosed that an attack by hackers exposed contact information of 76 million households and 7 million small businesses. "It's about firewall protection, it's about internal protection, it's about vendor protection, it's about everything that hooks up into you," stated Dimon. "There will be a lot of battles. Unfortunately some will be lost."

Consulting firm PwC (PricewaterhouseCoopers) stated that financial services companies will increase their cybersecurity spending by $2 billion over the next 2 years. PwC surveyed 758 banks, insurers, and other financial services companies, and stated they collectively spent $4.1 billion on cybersecurity in 2014.

According to an article in the *Wall Street Journal* from late 2014, Citigroup Inc.'s annual cybersecurity budget has risen to more than $300 million, and Wells Fargo spends roughly $250 million annually on cybersecurity.

8.2.2 General

The lifeblood of a banking or financial services firm is data, and these data include customer financials and account information, cardholder data and transactions, and nonpublic personal information. Almost all the information generated or used by a financial services firm is regulated, potentially sensitive, or private.

The data security compliance and regulation challenges alone are daunting. Data-at-rest protection requirements are found within PCI DSS requirements for credit card–related information, GLBA, SOX/J-SOX, NCUA, data privacy and data residency laws, and even the USA Patriot

Act. Each requirement adds to the need to protect sensitive information wherever it resides. In addition, organizations must meet the additional data security concerns that result from normal operations:

- Safeguarding critical financial data with maximum return and minimum risk

- Adjusting security postures as external attacks on financial infrastructure and online properties increase and change

- Meeting the need to protect from the traditional concerns with insiders and privileged users, while also dealing with the additional hazards that compromise of these accounts may bring

Digitized customer base

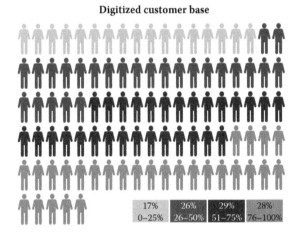

17%	26%	29%	28%
0–25%	26–50%	51–75%	76–100%

Cloud strategy according to digitized customer base

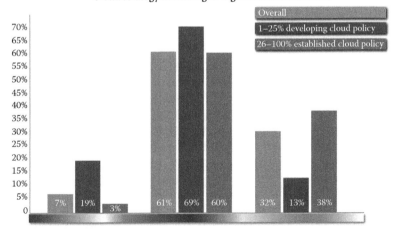

Cloud Strategy by digitalized base (CSA)

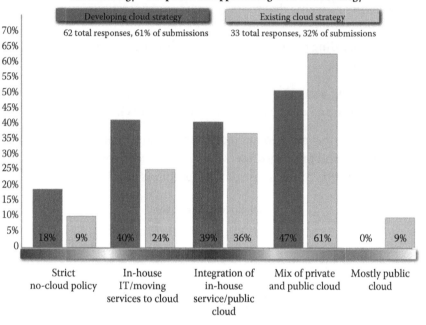

Cloud strategy—companies are approaching their cloud strategy

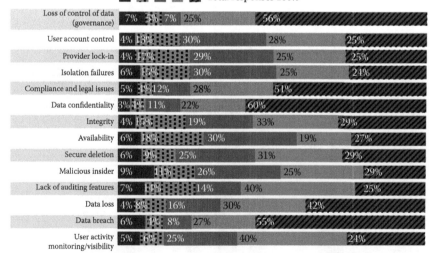

Cloud Computing security concerns ranked

Notable regulations

75%	63%	54%	47%	28%	26%	12%

| Data protection | Corporate governance | PCI-DSS | National regulations | GLBA | Basel 3 | PA-DSS |

Auditing	Auditing standards	Banking authorities	Cybersecurity framework	FDIC
FedRAMP	FFIEEC	GLBA	Insurance	IRS
ITAR	NIST	OSFI	Standards	SEC

8.3 HEALTHCARE

8.3.1 Vertical View

Healthcare cybersecurity is lagging behind other sectors. ABI Research says hospitals, clinics, trusts, and insurers are constantly under attack from malicious online agents, and yet the industry spends very little on cybersecurity, comparatively to other regulated critical industries. ABI Research calculates cybersecurity spending for healthcare protection will only reach $10 billion globally by 2020, just lower than 10% of total spend on critical infrastructure security.

The value of personal health information, made more easily available with the convergence to electronic health records, is 10 times that of financial data such as credit card numbers. Medical identity theft and fraud are also on the rise, and healthcare providers are struggling to cope instances of data breaches leaking millions of personal records. These findings are part of ABI Research's Cybersecurity Strategies for Critical Infrastructure Market Research.

"Cybersecurity for healthcare is still a small, fragmented market but the potential opportunities for expansion are large and will continue to grow as healthcare organizations increasingly come under cyberfire," says Michela Menting, ABI Research Digital Security Practice Director.

8.3.2 General

Healthcare organizations place their highest priorities around serving the needs of patients and the delivery of the care that they need, but at the same time, they operate within the limitations of a maze of regulatory and compliance requirements:

- HIPAA/HITECH: Meeting US Health Insurance Portability and Accountability Act (HIPAA) as well as Health Information Technology for Economic and Clinical Health Act (HITECH) requirements for safeguarding electronic Personal Healthcare Information (ePHI)

- Data breaches: Protecting their organizations from a violation of State, Federal, and Local data breach statutes

- EPCS: Meeting US Drug Enforcement Agency's (DEA) requirements for Electronic Prescriptions of Controlled Substances (EPCS)

- PCI DSS: Ensuring the security of payment transactions as required under the Payment Card Industry Data Security Standard (PCI DSS)

- FDA: Meeting US Food and Drug Administration (FDA) requirements for ensuring the trustworthiness and reliability of electronic records and signatures

Common to these requirement sets is the need to encrypt data-at-rest and implement secure access controls to the encrypted information. An additional safeguard to protect data-at-rest from data breaches is the incorporation of monitoring access patterns to protected data by those who use protected information as part of their work.

8.3.3 Retail Pharmacies

Retail pharmacies are in the uncomfortable position of needing to comply not only with PCI DSS standards but also with the need to

- Comply with HIPAA/HITECH security, privacy, and mandatory data breach disclosure rules for compromise of Electronic Patient Healthcare Information (EPHI)

- Protect their organizations from violation of State, Federal, and Local data breach statutes

- Meet US Drug Enforcement Agencies (DEA) requirements for Electronic Prescriptions of Controlled Substances (EPCS)

- Meet US Food and Drug Administration (FDA) requirements for ensuring the trustworthiness and reliability of electronic records and signatures

Consequently, retail pharmacies face not only the risk of financial forensic and credit monitoring costs and fines but also the likelihood of class-action lawsuits, new legal precedents, and an extraordinarily negative impact on long-term reputation, customer trust, and sales because of the very personal nature of patient healthcare information.

8.4 INFORMATION TECHNOLOGY OUTSOURCING

8.4.1 General

Outsourcing is a highly attractive strategy in today's economic environment and competitive global market. Enterprises outsource a variety of functions to third parties to reduce costs and time to market, free up resources to concentrate on core capabilities, and gain a competitive edge. Global outsourcing offers these substantial benefits but also poses some notable information security challenges.

The free flow of nonpublic information (NPI), customer confidential information (CCI), and intellectual property (IP) in the form of digital information such as source code, engineering drawings, personally identifiable information (PII), PCI compliance-affected data, and cardholder information has created a dilemma for companies that outsource—how do you safeguard digital information and still provide the access that outsourcing service providers need to get the job done?

Outsourcing is not simply the privilege of large corporations anymore either. Small and medium businesses are now taking advantage of this new opportunity to leverage economical outsourced resources. According to a study by *USA TODAY*, nearly 40% of start-ups outsource engineers, marketers, analysts, and others in jobs created in India and other nations.

Outsourcing raises information security concerns as enterprises need assurance that the information provided to an outsourcer is strongly protected from compromise. Outsourcing to the international market makes information security an even greater concern. Many of the tasks delegated to outsourcing service providers require companies to entrust their outsourcing partner with sensitive information. Sensitive personal information such as tax returns and credit card information tend to be top-of-mind in the public eye, but outsourcing also poses a costly threat to intellectual property. In outsourcing relationships, a company must often provide the outsourcing partner with access to vital IP assets, which are the key to the company's competitive edge. Exposing this valuable information to outsiders can pose significant security risks.

8.5 EDUCATION

8.5.1 General

Because of the nature of the content they keep and their varying locations, schools, universities, colleges, and other **educational institutions** are frequent victims of data breach. With research data, student and alumni personal records, health center records, payment information for tuitions, housing, food, and books, the **data security** needs of the education market are widespread. Beyond providing a secure environment for students and faculty, there are many government, industry, and state regulations that mandate data security for every type of information stored by educational institutions.

8.6 CYBERSECURITY CONSULTING SERVICE

Worldwide spending on information security will reach $71.1 billion in 2014, an increase of 7.9% over 2013, with the data loss prevention segment recording the fastest growth at 18.9%, according to the latest forecast from Gartner, Inc. Total information security spending will grow a further 8.2% in 2015 to reach $76.9 billion.

According to Gartner, the increasing adoption of mobile, cloud, social, and information (often interacting together) will drive use of new security technology and services through 2016.

"This Nexus of Forces is impacting security in terms of new vulnerabilities," said Gartner research director Lawrence Pingree. "It is also creating new opportunities to improve effectiveness, particularly as a result of better understanding security threats by using contextual information and other security intelligence."

Mr. Pingree said that the bigger trend that emerged in 2013 was the democratization of security threats, driven by the easy availability of malicious software (malware) and infrastructure (via the underground economy) that can be used to launch advanced targeted attacks.

"This has led to increased awareness among organizations that would have traditionally treated security as an IT function and a cost center," said Mr. Pingree.

Other trends in the information security market that form assumptions behind Gartner's latest forecast include the following:

- By 2015, roughly 10% of overall IT security enterprise product capabilities will be delivered in the cloud.

- A significant number of security markets are being affected by newly emerged delivery models. This is resulting in the growth of cloud-based security services, which are transforming, to different degrees, the way security is supplied and consumed by customers. While cloud-based services' competitive pricing puts pressure on the market, the cloud is also providing new growth opportunities, as some organizations switch from deploying on-premises products to cloud-based services or cloud-managed products. More than 30% of security controls deployed to the small or midsize business segment will be cloud based by 2015.

- Regulatory pressure will increase in Western Europe and Asia-Pacific from 2014.

- Regulatory compliance has been a major factor driving spending on security in the last 3 years, particularly in the United States. Gartner expects this influence to accelerate from 2014. Broader data privacy legislation such as the Australian Privacy Act is expected to sustain spending on security this year. Other examples of intensifying regulatory pressure driving spending on compliance include the issue of guidelines regarding personal information protection in China in February 2013 (although they are not legally binding) and planned implementation of an addition to the EU Data Protection Directive. Other examples include personal data protection laws (introduced in 2013) in Singapore and Malaysia.

- By year-end 2015, about 30% of infrastructure protection products will be purchased as part of a suite offering.

- The presence of highly mature and commoditizing technologies, such as EPP and e-mail security, will be contrasted by growth opportunities offered by segments such as SIEM, DLP, and emerging technologies within the "other security" segment. Security providers in the more mature and consolidated segments are predicted to support sales through the addition of new security controls as part of broader suite offerings. This will be the case within the EPP segment, with the increasing availability of DLP, mobile device management, vulnerability assessment, hosted archiving, and encryption for secure e-mail gateway. This expansion of suite offerings to include new security controls is expected to help maintain momentum and slow down commoditization of these mature markets.

- By 2018, more than half of organizations will use security services firms that specialize in data protection, security risk management, and security infrastructure management to enhance their security postures.

- Many organizations continue to lack the appropriate skills necessary to define, implement, and operate appropriate levels of data protection and privacy-specific security controls. This lack of skills leads organizations to contract security consulting firms that specialize in data protection and security risk management to address regulatory compliance demands and enhance their security postures. A significant portion of organizations are shifting existing resources away from the operational aspects of security technologies, such as security device administration and monitoring, toward mitigation and incident response. This new dynamic has given rise to significant growth throughout the globe for managed security services.

- Mobile security will be a higher priority for consumers from 2017 onward.

- There is a lack of penetration of security tools among users of new mobile platforms, and Gartner does not expect to see new demand for this type of capability to emerge before 2016. Most consumers do not recognize that antivirus is important on mobile devices and therefore have not yet established a consistent practice of buying mobile device endpoint protection software. This purchasing trend and market shift away from PCs will have significant repercussions on the consumer security market. However, as mobile devices gain in mass popularity and as security is likely to be a higher priority from 2017 onward, new market opportunities are likely to emerge.

8.7 GOVERNMENT/MILITARY

8.7.1 US Federal Sector

Federal sector provides new opportunities for small businesses and cybersecurity providers. Demand for vendor-furnished information security products and services by the US federal government will increase from $7.8 billion in fiscal year (FY) 2014 to $10.0 billion in 2019 at a compound annual growth rate of 5.2%, according to Deltek's Federal Information Security Market Report (published October 2014), which examines the trends and drivers shaping the federal information security marketplace and provides a forecast for the next 5 years.

President Obama's budget proposal for the 2016 FY includes a projected 10% increase in cybersecurity spend, reports Reuters. The total for 2016, if approved by Congress, will be $14 billion that will be spent across the US government to better protect private and federal networks from cyber threats.

Vice President Biden, Secretary of Energy Ernest Moniz, and White House Science Advisor John Holdren recently traveled to Norfolk State University in Norfolk, Virginia, to announce that the Department of Energy is providing a $25 million grant over the next 5 years to support cybersecurity education. The new grant will support the creation of a new cybersecurity consortium consisting of 13 Historically Black Colleges and Universities (HBCUs), two national labs, and a K–12 school district (source: whitehouse.gov).

The government is increasing its investments in advanced cybersecurity technologies. Special attention is being given to securing the Internet of Things through federally sponsored research in cyber-physical systems. Small businesses can use these R&D contractual vehicles to get involved in the government cybersecurity market.

The federal government has set aside special funds for small businesses to develop innovative solutions in cybersecurity. The government also requires large defense contractors to subcontract a certain percentage of their cybersecurity solutions development to small businesses. Thus, a small business has multiple avenues for engaging in the federal cybersecurity market, either through direct contract with the government or by helping a large business meet its small business subcontractor quota.

"To provide wider, discounted access to cybersecurity resources the General Services Administration (GSA) and the DHS are strategically sourcing cybersecurity tools and solutions through the Continuous Diagnostics and Mitigation (CDM) and Continuous Monitoring as a

Service (CMaaS) Blanket Purchase Agreements (BPAs) (see gsa.gov/cdm),"
says Dr. Anita D'Amico, CEO at Code Dx, developer of a software vulnerability assessment tool and listed at #15 on the Cybersecurity 500. Code
Dx has been awarded multiple SBIR grants from the DHS, totaling millions of dollars.

The US DHS budget is $38.2 billion for 2015. A total of $38.2 billion
in nondisaster, net discretionary budget authority is provided for DHS to
protect the nation from terrorist attacks, address critical capital needs, and
carry out core homeland security functions such as transportation security, cybersecurity, disaster preparedness, and border security (source:
whitehouse.gov).

The budget includes $549 million for supporting the EINSTEIN intru-
sion detection and prevention system and continuous diagnostics and
mitigation, key administration cybersecurity initiatives to address threats
and vulnerabilities against federal computer systems and networks. These
initiatives are conducted through the National Protection and Programs
Directorate, which protects federal computer systems and networks from
cyberattacks, disruptions, and exploitations; strengthens state and local
governments' cybersecurity capacity; and supports private sector efforts
to protect critical infrastructures (source: whitehouse.gov).

The budget also supports the design of a Federal Cyber Campus to colo-
cate key civilian cybersecurity agencies to promote a whole government
approach to cybersecurity incident response (source: whitehouse.gov).

The US National Intelligence Program budget is $45.6 billion for 2015.
A total of $45.6 billion in base discretionary funding is provided for the
National Intelligence Program to support national security goals and
reflect a deliberative process to focus funding on the most critical capabilities (source: whitehouse.gov).

The budget includes adapting to evolving cyberspace capabilities to
help protect federal networks, critical infrastructure, and America's economy, while improving the security of intelligence networks against intrusion and counterintelligence threats, and enhancing information sharing
through expanded use of the IT cloud to facilitate greater efficiency and
improved data security across the intelligence information environment
(source: whitehouse.gov).

8.7.1.1 Federal

During FY 2014, US-CERT processed more than 67,000 cybersecurity
incidents reported by CFO Act government agencies, up from the nearly

60,000 incidents reported in FY 2013, and the White House has made cybersecurity a top government-wide priority.

8.7.1.2 Insider Threats

Insider-implemented breaches, such as those by Edward Snowden and Bradley Manning, not only can severely cripple the ability of federal agencies to achieve their objectives but also can have a chilling effect on federal professional and administrative careers.

8.7.1.3 Stolen Credentials

While insider threats persist, external threats are becoming more menacing and sophisticated. Advanced persistent threats, or APTs, blur the line between insider and external threats by allowing external adversaries to steal the user credentials required to bypass perimeter defenses and act as insiders. Because of their sophistication and required resources, APTs are often attributed to nation-states and other highly organized entities.

8.7.1.4 The Need for Compliance

As cybersecurity threats have proliferated and computer technology has advanced, compliance has become increasingly complex.

The government mandates encryption, and major regulations such as NIST 800-53, FIPs (up to level 3), and Common Criteria need to be part of any data-security solution, and, as data move to the cloud, agencies need to comply with FedRAMP. Finally, depending on the agency, HIPAA-HITECH and PCI DSS may also be important.

8.7.1.5 Controlling Costs and Risk

Government agencies have a significant task at hand with ever-decreasing IT budgets. This is in dark contrast to a need to bolster security measures to prevent and mitigate cyber breaches. The Vormetric platform provides the federal government a unified platform for data protection across the enterprise with a single strategy for data security. This eliminates disconnected, stovepiped solutions. Moreover, it provides concise information that protects data and informs security personnel of the actions and behaviors of its users and malicious use of valid credentials. Organizations employing this unified enterprise strategy are finding a compelling ROI (return on investment) that eliminates point solutions for encryption from hardware and application vendors and measures to reduce physical separation of storage. Your data are more secure and both the complexity of managing the data and costs are reduced.

8.7.1.6 Civilian Agencies

Managers of federal civilian agencies face a dizzying array of data security needs general to all government agencies and departments and specific to those dealing with civilian issues:

These agencies and departments are faced with

- Insider threats, such as those illustrated by Snowden and Manning
- Stolen credentials and APTs
- The need to comply with federal mandates and regulations
- The need for scalability
- The need to move to the cloud

But perhaps more specific to these civilian agencies are the needs for

- Securing civilian personal identification information (PII)
- Securing personal healthcare information
- Protecting data that affect our critical infrastructure, such as those involved in managing the flow of energy, water, food, financial, and political resources that affect the lives of our citizens at a local and national level

8.7.1.7 Defense

The Department of Defense has challenges of sharing critical data related to mission, supply chain, finance, and personnel across departments as well as with coalition partners. This does not come without risk and presents multiple opportunities for cyberattacks to capitalize on vulnerabilities to access critical data that may affect mission success or the lives of our warfighters.

These agencies and departments are faced with

- Insider threats, such as those illustrated by Snowden and Manning
- Stolen credentials and APTs

- The need to comply with federal mandates and regulations

- The need for large-scale deployments as well as tactical agile compute environments

- The need to move to the cloud while maintaining data center operations

- The information driving missions needs to be secured, several key examples would be as follows:

  - Forward deployed IT at the theater edge

  - Mobile field units, including drones and other hardware

- Allowing secure access to data across communities of interest in a Big Data environment

- Large amounts of PII and PHI

- Data center consolidation (joint information environment [JIE] and joint regional security stack [JRSS]) are affecting decisions relative to consolidation

- Closing "air gaps" in storage infrastructure to reduce risk and mobility during mission

Moreover, data managers in the Defense community must do all this in tight time frames and budgets.

8.7.1.8 Intelligence Community

The US Intelligence Community shares many data security concerns with other federal agencies, but they also have some that are unique to their mission.

Not only are these agencies faced with

- Insider threats, such as those illustrated by Snowden and Manning

- Stolen credentials and APTs

- The need to comply with federal mandates and regulations

- The need for scalability

- The need to move to the cloud

They also need to manage highly sensitive data in a secure manner in several scenarios:

- Forward deployed, autonomous servers
- Data sharing with other intelligence agencies, but with user controlled data constraints
- Data center consolidation
- Multitenant, multicloud environments

Moreover, data managers in the intelligence community must do all this in tight time frames and budgets.

8.7.2 State and Local

State and local government agencies in the United States rely on sensitive information stored in databases and file servers and processed by various applications to provide their essential services. Almost every state has enacted a **data breach notification** law. These government data security laws generally require government agencies and businesses that have personal information about residents within a state to notify those residents of any unauthorized access to their information.

Government agencies are expected to protect personally identifiable information. Protection of such information is an integral part of demonstrating good stewardship and to comply with **state data breach** and **data protection** legislation.

8.7.2.1 State Security Breach Disclosure Laws

Forty-six US states, the District of Columbia, Puerto Rico, and the Virgin Islands have enacted legislation requiring notification of security breaches involving personal information.

State	Disclosure of Breach of Security Legislation
Alaska	Alaska Stat. § 45.48.010 et seq.
Arizona	Ariz. Rev. Stat. § 44-7501
Arkansas	Ark. Code § 4-110-101 et seq.
California	Cal. Civ. Code §§ 56.06, 1785.11.2, 1798.29, 1798.82

(*Continued*)

State	Disclosure of Breach of Security Legislation
Colorado	Colo. Rev. Stat. § 6-1-716
Connecticut	Conn. Gen Stat. 36a-701(b)
Delaware	Del. Code tit. 6, § 12B-101 et seq.
Florida	Fla. Stat. § 817.5681
Georgia	Ga. Code §§ 10-1-910, -911
Hawaii	Haw. Rev. Stat. § 487N-2
Idaho	Idaho Stat. §§ 28-51-104 to 28-51-107
Illinois	815 ILCS 530/1 et seq.
Indiana	Ind. Code §§ 24-4.9 et seq., 4-1-11 et seq.
Iowa	Iowa Code § 715C.1
Kansas	Kan. Stat. 50-7a01, 50-7a02
Louisiana	La. Rev. Stat. § 51:3071 et seq.
Maine	Me. Rev. Stat. tit. 10 §§ 1347 et seq.
Maryland	Md. Code, Com. Law § 14-3501 et seq.
Massachusetts	Mass. Gen. Laws § 93H-1 et seq.
Michigan	Mich. Comp. Laws § 445.72
Minnesota	Minn. Stat. §§ 325E.61, 325E.64
Mississippi	2010 H.B. 583 (effective July 1, 2011)
Missouri	Mo. Rev. Stat. § 407.1500
Montana	Mont. Code §§ 30-14-1704, 2-6-504
Nebraska	Neb. Rev. Stat. §§ 87-801, -802, -803, -804, -805, -806, -807
Nevada	Nev. Rev. Stat. 603A.010 et seq.
New Hampshire	N.H. Rev. Stat. §§ 359-C:19, -C:20, -C:21
New Jersey	N.J. Stat. 56:8-163
New York	N.Y. Gen. Bus. Law § 899-aa
North Carolina	N.C. Gen. Stat § 75-65
North Dakota	N.D. Cent. Code § 51-30-01 et seq.
Ohio	Ohio Rev. Code §§ 1347.12, 1349.19, 1349.191, 1349.192
Oklahoma	Okla. Stat. § 74-3113.1 and § 24-161 to -166
Oregon	Oregon Rev. Stat. § 646A.600 et seq.
Pennsylvania	73 Pa. Stat. § 2303
Rhode Island	R.I. Gen. Laws § 11-49.2-1 et seq.
South Carolina	S.C. Code § 39-1-90
Tennessee	Tenn. Code § 47-18-2107, 2010 S.B. 2793
Texas	Tex. Bus. & Com. Code § 521.03
Utah	Utah Code §§ 13-44-101, 13-44-102, 13-44-201, 13-44-202, 13-44-301
Vermont	Vt. Stat. tit. 9 § 2430 et seq.
Virginia	Va. Code § 18.2-186.6, § 32.1-127.1:05 (effective January 1, 2011)

(Continued)

State	Disclosure of Breach of Security Legislation
Washington	Wash. Rev. Code § 19.255.010, 42.56.590
West Virginia	W.V. Code §§ 46A-2A-101 et seq.
Wisconsin	Wis. Stat. § 134.98 et seq.
Wyoming	Wyo. Stat. § 40-12-501 to -502
District of Columbia	D.C. Code § 28- 3851 et seq.
Puerto Rico	10 Laws of Puerto Rico § 4051 et. seq.
Virgin Islands	V.I. Code § 2208

Note: States with no security breach law: Alabama, Kentucky, New Mexico, and South Dakota.

CHAPTER 9

Application Security
by Industry*

9.1 POLICY COMPLIANCE

The Open Web Application Security Project (OWASP) is a community consensus compilation of the most important web application vulnerabilities. The OWASP Top 10 is often referenced by industry standards such as PCI-DSS, which sets forth security standards for payment card processing systems. In analyzing application security policy compliance across multiple industries, the study by Veracode rated compliance on the basis of applications being free of OWASP Top 10 vulnerabilities as found by static analysis, dynamic analysis, or manual penetration testing. Key observations include the following:

- Low pass rate for the OWASP Top 10 policy

- A wide variability in this pass rate by industry vertical

  - High first-assessment OWASP compliance rate for applications in financial services driven by disproportionate use of Java or .NET, impact of regulatory mandates, and a focus on continuous improvement processes

---

* STATE OF SOFTWARE SECURITY Volume 6: Focus on Industry Verticals JUNE 2015 https://www.veracode.com/sites/default/files/Resources/Reports/state-software-security-report-june-2015-report.pdf.

- Low pass rate in government possibly attributed to higher use of scripting languages and more prevalent use of older languages that are known to produce more vulnerabilities

- Low pass rate in healthcare possibly driven by lack of regulatory demands

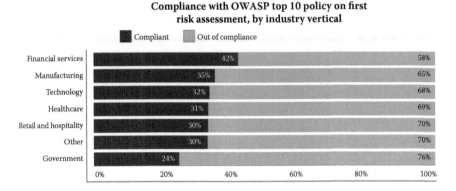

Compliance with OWASP top 10 policy on first risk assessment, by industry vertical

9.2 INTERNALLY VERSUS EXTERNALLY DEVELOPED APPLICATIONS

Research data consistently show that commercial software applications are not significantly more secure than those internally developed. This observation is independent of the specific industry vertical. Commercial software had a 9% lower OWASP pass rate than internally developed software possible because of the broader mix of software languages used for commercial software and the age of the code base.

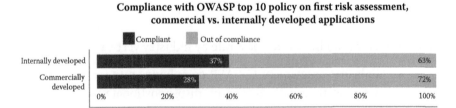

Compliance with OWASP top 10 policy on first risk assessment, commercial vs. internally developed applications

9.3 APPLICATION FLAW DENSITY

Application flaw density measures average risk per unit of software found by conducting a binary static analysis of the code. This approach finds potential vulnerabilities caused by developer errors. It is defined as the number of flaws for an application divided by the size of the application's executable code in megabytes. In the case of uncompilable scripting languages such as JavaScript, PHP, or Classic ASP, the density is measured in terms of the size of the source code in megabytes. Flaw density normalizes out application size and only includes static assessment flaws. In this way, it allows a side-by-side comparison of application risk. This metric was only calculated on study applications that had a static analysis conducted. Flaw density is also affected by operational factors such as the types and mix of programming languages in use within an organization. Observations include the following:

- The highest observed average flaw density is in the manufacturing industry vertical likely explained by disproportionately high ColdFusion applications.

- Technology had the third highest flaw density possibly explained by a disproportionately high share of C/C++ applications.

- The average flaw density in healthcare is lower than any other industry.

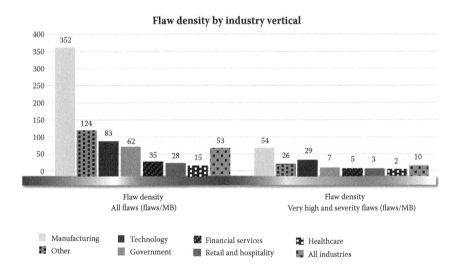

Flaw density by industry vertical

9.4 APPLICATION REMEDIATION

Application remediation is the number of vulnerabilities fixed within a given industry as a percentage of the total number of vulnerabilities found. Manufacturing vertical is exceptionally good at addressing this issue. This may be attributed to this industry's broad adoption of process improvement methodologies as part of its culture. Manufacturing has also been a leader in implementing supply chain controls for its critical suppliers. As supply chain becomes increasingly important in digital commerce, other industries may adopt these techniques as well. Differences in security policy can also drive significant differences in security program performance. This can easily be seen by how policies that require a large number of vulnerability categories seem to discourage developer participation, which paradoxically make the organization less secure. Observations include the following:

- Manufacturing and financial services fix the largest percentage of flaws.

- Government fixes the lowest percentage of flaws.

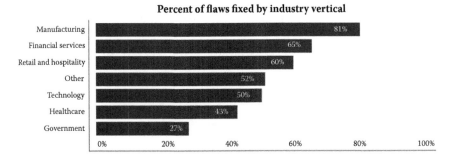

9.5 HIGH-PROFILE VULNERABILITIES

The four most important vulnerability categories are SQL injection, cross-site scripting, cryptography issues, and command injection. This is attributed to their pervasiveness and severity, specifically:

- SQL injection was the application vulnerability most often exploited in web application attacks in the 2015 Verizon Data Breach Incident.

- Cross-site scripting is overall far more prevalent than any other category.

- OS command injection played a role in 2014's Shellshock vulnerability, in which a commonly used open source component was exploited in a way that allowed taking over a server to run an arbitrary code.

- Cryptography issues are highly prevalent across all applications and may be used to allow an attacker to retrieve poorly protected data or hijack communication with an application.

Consistent with their low pass rate for the OWASP Top 10, the government industry vertical has the highest prevalence of both SQL injection and cross-site scripting, while organizations in retail and hospitality have the lowest. Among other flaw categories, organizations in healthcare have the highest incidence of cryptographic issues. This is true despite the strict data confidentiality requirements for personal information imposed by Health Insurance Portability and Accountability Act (HIPAA).

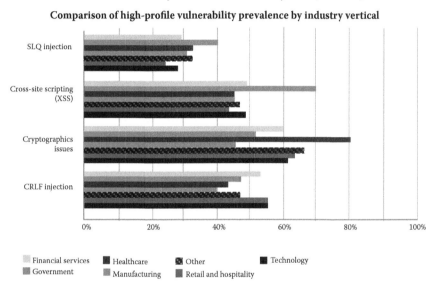

Comparison of high-profile vulnerability prevalence by industry vertical

CHAPTER 10

Cloud Computing and Cybersecurity Education Challenges

10.1 INDUSTRY VERTICAL KNOWLEDGE

While information technology (IT) is the ubiquitous horizontal layer underlying all industry sector verticals, implementation specifics are strongly influenced by security requirements. A recent study of Cloud Computing adoption highlighted this by documenting the difference between regulated and unregulated industries (Kimberly Harris-Ferrante 2014).

10.1.1 Regulated Industries

Insurance: Private clouds are preferred because they are more secure than public clouds. By 2015, industry association community clouds are expected to increase in popularity.

Banking: In the banking industry, the main concern is that a cloud environment is not secure enough. This issue drives cloud use in this particular industry toward administrative functions such as e-mail, file sharing, and sharing of notes.

Government: While opportunities to use Cloud Computing in a variety of ways do exist, it is also misunderstood. Today, the biggest opportunities are in public Cloud Computing, but many in this industry fear security problems.

10.1.2 Unregulated Industries

Retail: In this industry, cloud implementations have been mostly Infrastructure as a Service (IaaS) or Platform as a Service (PaaS) solutions. Security, availability, and vendor maturity are all aspects that retailers consider when deciding which functions they want deployed from the cloud.

Media: Audiences today can access content of any form in a variety of ways. This is why service providers and application developers are exploring a cloud-based visual way to enable multiscreen entertainment.

Manufacturing: This industry uses the cloud for logistics, sales support functions, human resources (HR), product development, and life cycle management, as well as some manufacturing operations.

10.2 A GLOBAL CYBERSECURITY VIEW

Globalization of commerce driven by ubiquitous and real-time Internet-based interactions makes a global perspective on security paramount. International health IT, for example, currently supports the move toward Cloud Computing with governments, industry leaders, and advocacy groups keen to adopt cloud-based solutions in healthcare. The potential benefits, however, need to be evaluated against the significant cyber-related risks. As shown in a recent comparative study on US and European Union (EU) health professionals, views on the potential benefits and risks from Cloud Computing vary greatly (Wendy Currie 2014). The results from surveying healthcare organizations in the United States and five EU countries (France, Germany, the Netherlands, Sweden, and the United Kingdom) identify differences across countries in health IT policy, incentives for adoption, privacy and security, and trust in third-party suppliers. The findings show that privacy and security are important issues for healthcare organizations, yet differences exist between the United States and across EU Member States in how these concepts are viewed. The study provides instructive insights on cross-jurisdictional approaches to personal data and privacy, regulations and rules on health data export, how countries interpret and implement different data protection regulations and rules, and the practical implementation of regulatory rules.

A key challenge for international governments keen to promote the use of advanced IT across all industry verticals is to provide an effective legal and regulatory framework that governs trans-border data flows. In today's internationally interconnected world, personal data are likely to be held on servers that may be located in legal and regulatory jurisdictions outside the country where the data are collected and used. This is not simply an "IT challenge" for the business community, since the ramifications need to be understood and addressed within the context of the legal and regulatory framework that governs potential trans-border data flows. Cybersecurity professionals will be asked to provide direction and guidance to policymakers, regulators, and industry leaders.

Despite the risk, the trend toward increasing trans-border data flows will continue, albeit with serious concerns about privacy and security. Data also suggest that many organizations are concerned about working with third-party providers in the pursuit of these advanced capabilities. While this may be a trust issue, it may also stem from concerns about how to develop and execute sufficiently robust legal contracts. Corporate users are likely to enter into standard contractual clauses with IT providers, which may not fully protect the rights of all parties, including the individuals whose personal data are being stored. Unlike previous technology, which resided within a single organization, today's business landscape inevitably includes the potential for trans-border data flows across multiple legal and regulatory jurisdictions.

10.3 GLOBAL LEGAL FRAMEWORK KNOWLEDGE

The lack of a consistent legal and regulatory environment shines a harsh spotlight on cyberspace. Our cybersecurity workforce must be educated on how to interpret international policies with respect to their own organizational policies, industry regulations, national laws, and, eventually, international protocols. As a start, these professionals should be taught to evaluate IT operations across these seven Business Software Alliance recommended areas:

> Ensuring privacy: Buttressing users' faith that their information will not be used or disclosed in unexpected ways. At the same time, to maximize the benefit of advanced IT, providers must be free to move data internationally in the most efficient way.

Promoting security: Users must be assured that IT providers understand and properly manage the risks inherent in storing and running applications in cyberspace. Solution providers must be able to implement cutting-edge cybersecurity solutions without being required to use specific technologies.

Battling cybercrime: In cyberspace, as in the real world, laws must provide meaningful deterrence and clear causes of action. Legal systems should provide an effective mechanism for law enforcement, and for IT providers themselves, to combat unauthorized access to data stored on interconnected global platforms.

Protecting intellectual property: In order to promote continued innovation and technological advancement, intellectual property laws should provide for clear protection and vigorous enforcement against misappropriation and infringement of the developments that underlie the IT industry.

Ensuring data portability and the harmonization of international rules: The smooth flow of data around the world requires efforts to promote openness and interoperability. Governments should work with industry to develop standards, while also working to minimize conflicting legal obligations on IT providers.

Promoting free trade: By its very nature, Internet-based technologies operate across national boundaries. The ability to promote economic growth depends on a global market that transcends barriers to free trade, including preferences for particular products or providers.

Establishing the necessary IT infrastructure: International commerce requires robust, ubiquitous, and affordable broadband access. This can be achieved through policies that provide incentives for private sector investment in broadband infrastructure and laws that promote universal access to broadband (Business Software Alliance 2013).

The cyber workforce needs to also be internationally savvy in order to deal with global scenarios. Geo-specific IT security policies and procedures will become the norm rather than the exception (i.e., stronger identification and access management challenges for users accessing from Pakistan). Important educational topics will include the following:

- Multinational enterprise risk management

- International cyber event management

- Industrialized criminal activity/multinational fraud

- Cloud-enabled thieves and terrorist

10.4 CISO TRAINING, EDUCATION, AND CERTIFICATION

According to primary research conducted for this text, most enterprise chief information security officers (CISOs) have 8 years of experience in their position and has complemented a formal master's degree with multiple security-related certifications. Formal and "on the job training" has provided them with a broad range of hard and soft skill sets including industry business knowledge, communications skills, and relationship building. As the organization's cybersecurity executive, this mix appears to be critical to future success.

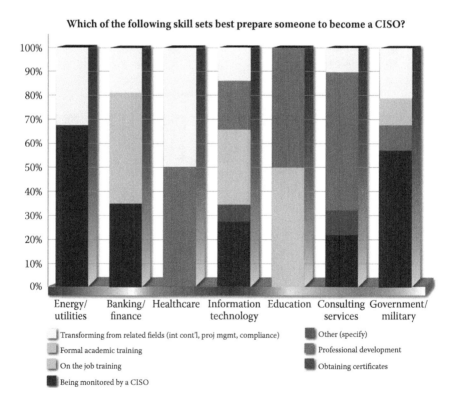

Which of the following skill sets best prepare someone to become a CISO?

Which of the following skill sets best prepare someone to become a CISO?

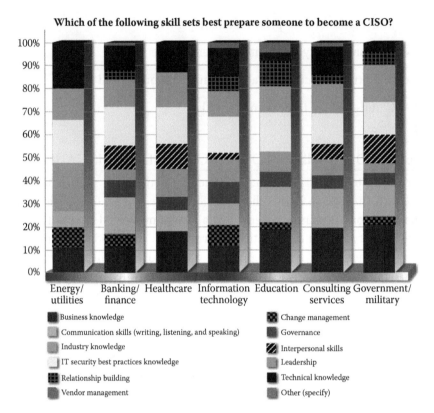

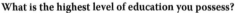

What is the highest level of education you possess?

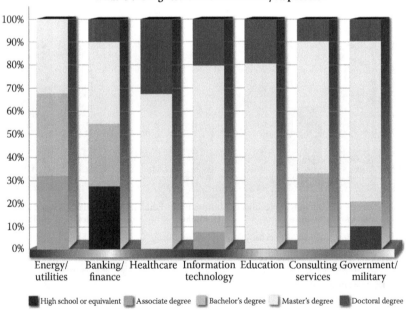

Which of the following certifications do you possess?

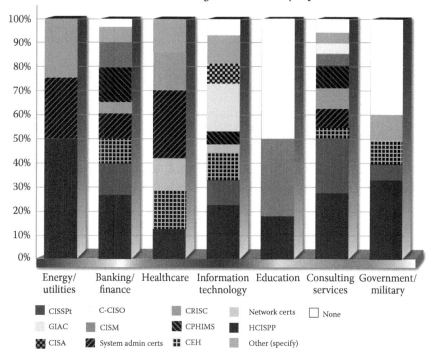

Which of the following certifications do you think a CISO should possess?

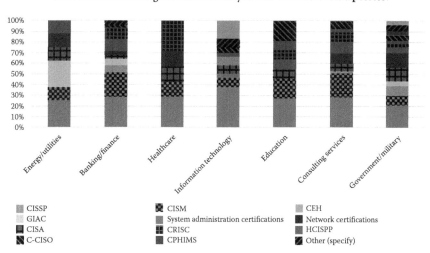

10.5 HYBRID IT INFRASTRUCTURE MANAGEMENT

The cybersecurity workforce will need to learn how to operate and securely collaborate in a de-perimeterized world. This means more training in hybrid IT infrastructure design, governance, and operations, and use of new models like "Cloud Cube" reference model (The Open Group: Jericho Forum 2009).

The Jericho Forum is an international group of organizations working together to define and promote the solutions surrounding the issue of de-perimeterization. It was officially founded at the offices of the Open Group in Reading, UK, on January 16, 2004. It had existed as a loose affiliation of interested corporate CISOs discussing the topic since the summer of 2003. One of the earlier outputs of the group is a position paper entitled "The Jericho Forum Commandments," which are a set of principles that describe how best to survive in a de-perimeterized world. The paper outlined an initial analysis process that started with the classification of data with respect to sensitivity and regulatory compliance in order to know which protection rules would be appropriate for application. A second requirement is to operate within an environment of universally adopted standards for data classification, trust level management, and standardized metadata representation for cloud security. Once these prerequisites are met, managers and operators could then be able to make rational decisions about the following:

- What data and processes should be moved to the cloud
- The appropriate service models (IaaS, PaaS, and Software as a Service [SaaS]) for relevant operational and business process
- The most appropriate "Cloud Formation" to use

The Jericho Forum identified four criteria to differentiate cloud formations from each other and the manner of their provision. The Cloud Cube Model summarizes these four dimensions:

Dimension: Internal (I)/External (E)

- If it is within your own physical boundary, then it is internal.
- If it is not within your own physical boundary, then it is external.

Dimension: Proprietary (P)/Open (O)

- Proprietary means that the organization providing the service is keeping the means of provision under their ownership. As a result, when operating in clouds that are proprietary, you may not be able to move to another cloud supplier without significant effort or investment. Often, the more innovative technology advances occur in the proprietary domain. As such, the proprietor may choose to enforce restrictions through patents and by keeping the technology involved a trade secret.

- Clouds that are open are using technology that is not proprietary, meaning that there are likely to be more suppliers, and you are not as constrained in being able to share your data and collaborate with selected parties using the same open technology. Open services tend to be those that are widespread and consumerized, and most likely a published open standard, for example, e-mail (SMTP).

Dimension: Perimeterized (Per)/De-perimeterized (D-p) Architectures

- Perimeterized implies continuing to operate within the traditional IT perimeter, often signaled by "network firewalls." As has been discussed in previous published Jericho Forum papers, this approach inhibits collaboration. In effect, when operating in the perimeterized areas, you may simply extend your own organization's perimeter into the external Cloud Computing domain using a VPN and operating the virtual server in your own IP domain, making use of your own directory services to control access. Then, when the computing task is completed, you can withdraw your perimeter back to its original traditional position. We consider this type of system perimeter to be a traditional, though a virtual, perimeter.

- De-perimeterized assumes that the system perimeter is architected following the principles outlined in the Jericho Forum's Commandments and Collaboration Oriented Architectures Framework. The terms *micro-perimeterization* and *macro-perimeterization* will likely be in active use here—for example, in a de-perimeterized frame, the data would be encapsulated with metadata and mechanisms that would protect the data from inappropriate usage. COA-enabled systems allow secure collaboration. In a de-perimeterized environment, an organization can collaborate securely with selected parties (business partner, customer, supplier, outworker) globally over any COA capable network.

Dimension: Insourced/Outsourced

- Insourced: the service is provided by your own staff under your control.

- Outsourced: the service is provided by a third party (The Open Group: Jericho Forum 2009).

Although the Jericho Model was designed specifically for Cloud Computing, it also provides an excellent framework for addressing today's hybrid IT infrastructures environment. Organizations will need to develop policies that address every facet of the cube and cybersecurity professionals will be called upon to monitor and enforce those policies.

10.6 RISK MANAGEMENT FRAMEWORKS

Global economic stability and the integrity of governmental services will largely depend on cybersecurity, so our workforce must be educated on the use and application of risk estimation metrics. "Quantitative risk analysis aspires to cede precise numeric monetary values to assets. It designates the financial risk of threats impact and frequency, costs of control and loss" (Latifa Ben Arfa Rabaia 2014). Some of the more relevant risk management frameworks include the following:

- Single loss expectancy (SLE)—The SLE is the expected monetary loss every time a risk occurs. It is calculated by multiplying asset value (AV) with exposure factor (EF) as shown in formula SLE = AV*EF, where AV is the financial value of the asset and EF is expressed within a range from 0% to 100% and that an asset's value will be destroyed by risk (Tsiakis 2010).

- Annual loss expectancy (ALE)—The ALE is the expected cumulative cost of risk over a period of 1 year. It is defined as the cost (loss in monetary units) of the damage resulted by a failure multiplied by its frequency in a period of 1 year: ALE = SLE*ARO, where the annual rate of occurrence (ARO) is the probability that a risk will occur in this particular period of 1 year (Boehme 2008).

- OCTAVE (Operationally Critical Threat, Asset, and Vulnerability Evaluation)—OCTAVE is a risk-based strategic assessment and planning technique for security that was developed by the Software Engineering Institute of Carnegie Mellon University in the United States (Mayer 2009). The method's aims are examining organizational and technological issues as well as defining an organization's security strategy and plan. It consists of three steps: making files of threat scenarios based on assets, recognizing the vulnerabilities of major facilities, and assessing the risk and developing security strategies.

- CRAMM (CCTA Risk Analysis and Management Method)—The CRAMM method was developed in 1985 by the Central Computer and Telecommunications Agency of the UK government (Mayer 2009). The methodological part of CRAMM is composed of three steps:

  - The first step identifies assets, which are divided into three classes: physical, software, and data. The valuation of assets is generally done in terms of the impact coming from information potentially being unavailable, destroyed, disclosed, or modified for software and data. This estimation of assets may be done in a quantitative way by valuing them in financial terms by data owners (the business unit managers).

  - The second step identifies and estimates the level of threats and vulnerabilities and provides some mapping between threats and assets and between threats and impacts in a qualitative way.

  - The third step produces a set of countermeasures that are considered as necessary to manage the identified risks.

- Information security risk management framework for Cloud Computing environments—A qualitative information risk management framework for better understanding critical areas of focus in Cloud Computing environments and identifying threats and vulnerabilities. The qualitative risk analysis proposed method is used to approach risk assessment and rank severity of threats by using classes of probabilities such as low, medium, and high, and damages for cloud providers (Zhang 2010).

- MFC—A quantitative infrastructure that estimates the security of a system. The model measures the security of a system in terms of the loss that each stakeholder stands to sustain as a result of security breakdowns. The infrastructure in question reflects the values that stakeholders have in each security requirement, the dependency of security requirements on the operation of architectural components, and the impact of those security threats (A. Ben Aissa 2010).

10.7 KEY EDUCATIONAL TOPICS: CRITICAL THREATS TO CLOUD SECURITY

With Cloud Computing dominating business IT, the cybersecurity workforce should have much more focused education on addressing the following nine critical threats to cloud security (Cloud Security Alliance 2013):

Data breaches—Sensitive internal data fall into the hands of competitors. While data loss and data leakage are both serious threats to Cloud Computing, the measures put in place to mitigate one of these threats can exacerbate the other. You may be able to encrypt your data to reduce the impact of a data breach, but if you lose your encryption key, you will lose your data as well. Conversely, you may decide to keep offline backups of your data to reduce the impact of a catastrophic data loss, but this increases your exposure to data breaches.

Data loss—Permanently losing data. Under the new EU data protection rules, data destruction and corruption of personal data are considered forms of data breaches and would require appropriate notifications. Many compliance policies require organizations to retain audit records or other documentation. If an organization stores this data in the cloud, its loss could jeopardize the organization's compliance status.

Account hijacking—Attack methods such as phishing, fraud, and exploitation of software vulnerabilities still achieve results. Credentials and passwords are often reused, which amplifies the impact of such attacks. Account and service hijacking, usually with stolen credentials, remains a top threat. With stolen credentials, attackers can often access critical areas of deployed Cloud Computing services, allowing them to compromise the confidentiality, integrity, and availability of those services. Organizations should be aware of these techniques as well as common defense in-depth protection strategies to contain the damage (and possible litigation) resulting from a breach. Organizations should look to prohibit the sharing of account credentials between users and services, and leverage strong two-factor authentication techniques where possible.

Insecure APIs—Cloud Computing providers expose a set of software interfaces or APIs that customers use to manage and interact with cloud services. Provisioning, management, orchestration, and monitoring are all performed using these interfaces. The security and availability of general cloud services are dependent on the security of these basic APIs. While most providers strive to ensure that security is well integrated into their service models, it is critical for consumers of those services to understand the security implications associated with the usage, management, orchestration, and monitoring of cloud services. Reliance on a weak set of interfaces and APIs exposes organizations to a variety of security issues related to confidentiality, integrity, availability, and accountability.

Denial of service—Denial-of-service attacks are attacks meant to prevent users of a cloud service from being able to access their data or their applications. There is the possibility that an attacker may not be able to completely knock your service off of the net, but may still cause it to consume so much processing time that it becomes too expensive for you to run and you will be forced to take it down yourself.

Malicious insiders—The risk of malicious insiders has been debated in the security industry. While the level of threat is left to debate, the fact of the insider threat being a real adversary is not. From IaaS to PaaS and SaaS, the malicious insider has increasing levels of access to more critical systems, and eventually to data. Systems that depend solely on the cloud service provider (CSP) for security are at great risk. Even if encryption is implemented, if the keys are not kept with the customer and are only available at data-usage time, the system is still vulnerable to malicious insider attack.

Abuse of cloud services—It might take an attacker years to crack an encryption key using his own limited hardware, but using an array of cloud servers, he might be able to crack it in minutes. Alternately, he might use that array of cloud servers to stage a DDoS attack, serve malware, or distribute pirated software. This threat is more of an issue for CSPs than cloud consumers, but it does raise a number of serious implications for those providers. How will you detect people abusing your service? How will you define abuse? How will you prevent them from doing it again?

Insufficient due diligence—Too many enterprises jump into the cloud without understanding the full scope of the undertaking. Without a complete understanding of the CSP environment, applications, or services that are being pushed to the cloud, and operational responsibilities such as incident response, encryption, and security monitoring, organizations are taking on unknown levels of risk in ways they may not even comprehend, but that are a far departure from their current risks. An organization that rushes to adopt cloud technologies subjects itself to a number of issues. Contractual issues arise over obligations to liability, response, or transparency by creating mismatched expectations between the CSP and the customer. Pushing applications that are dependent on "internal" network-level security controls to the cloud is dangerous when those controls disappear or do not match the customer's expectation. Unknown operational and architectural issues arise when designers and architects unfamiliar with cloud technologies are designing applications being pushed to the cloud. The bottom line for enterprises and organizations moving to a cloud technology model is that they must have capable resources and perform extensive internal and CSP due diligence to understand the risks they assume by adopting this new technology model. This threat is specifically attributed to lack of education (note: low level of perceived risk and a high level of actual risk).

Shared technology issues—CSPs deliver their services in a scalable way by sharing infrastructure, platforms, and applications. Whether it is the underlying components that make up this infrastructure (e.g., CPU caches, GPUs, etc.) that were not designed to offer strong isolation properties for a multitenant architecture (IaaS), redeployable platforms (PaaS), or multicustomer applications (SaaS), the threat of shared vulnerabilities exists in all delivery models. A compromise of an integral piece of shared technology—such as the hypervisor, a shared platform component, or an application in a SaaS environment—exposes more than just the compromised customer;

rather, it exposes the entire environment to a potential of compromise and breach. This vulnerability is dangerous because it potentially can affect an entire cloud at once.

10.8 NEXT STEPS FOR EDUCATING THE CYBERSECURITY WORKFORCE

There are a myriad of additional new threat vectors that will comprise supplemental educational needs for new cybersecurity workers. Some of these include the following:

IT supply chain management—Many of the components—including hardware, firmware, and software—that make up a technological product contain elements stemming from a broad global market that includes nations as diverse as Germany, China, India, Brazil, and Japan. This makes it very difficult to ascertain the complete security of an end product. The market for technological goods and components grows every year and the need for cyber supply chain security grows with it.

Shadow IT—Employees now bring their own laptops, tablets, and smartphones to the workplace. This means that administrators are tasked with managing applications of unknown origin and inadequate security standards. Referred to as "shadow IT," the use of these alternative resources is mostly done simply out of convenience. Many of these efforts are coordinated in an effort to gain productivity advantages and streamline daily tasks. Public cloud services, for example, are often leveraged without permission of IT teams, as staff members tend to use these tools to collaborate and share files. Although shadow IT is generally aligned with overarching business goals, organizational security standards are typically ignored.

Critical civil infrastructure—The critical infrastructure community includes public and private owners and operators, and other supporting entities that play a role in securing the nation's infrastructure. Each sector performs critical functions that are supported by IT, industrial control systems (ICS), and, in many cases, both IT and ICS. To manage cybersecurity risks, the National Institute of Standards and Technology has developed a cybersecurity framework designed to help professionals understand and address the security challenges and considerations specific to IT and ICS. The framework is a risk-based approach composed of three parts: the Framework Core, the Framework Profile, and the Framework Implementation Tiers. This information should be used by organizations to determine the acceptable level of risk for IT and ICS assets and systems (National Institute of Standards and Technologies 2013).

Corporate social media—Conducting business and social life today inevitably involves the sharing of information. Companies outsource their business processes to partners, data and applications are moved to Cloud Computing–based platforms, and social media has been embraced as a convenient and effective means of communication with customers and collaboration with suppliers. These changes not only increase the potential for data loss but also open organizations to the threat of infiltration and attack from the outside.

Cloud service brokerage—A cloud server broker is a third party that acts as an intermediary between the purchaser of a Cloud Computing service and the sellers of that service. As these services proliferate, organizations are often using brokers to help in the transition. In the cybersecurity realm, this is yet another attack vector that must be evaluated and analyzed.

Internet of things—The ability to connect, communicate with, and remotely manage an incalculable number of networked, automated devices via the Internet is becoming pervasive. As organizations and individuals become increasingly reliant on intelligent, interconnected devices, cybersecurity professionals will be called upon to protect them from intrusions and interference that could compromise personal privacy or threaten public safety.

Personal mobile devices—Smartphone and personal digital assistant security has not kept pace with traditional computer security. Technical security measures, such as firewalls, antivirus, and encryption, are uncommon on mobile phones, and mobile phone operating systems are not updated as frequently as those on personal computers. Malicious software can make a mobile phone a member of a network of devices that can be controlled by an attacker (a "botnet"). Malicious software can also send device information to attackers and perform other harmful commands. Mobile phones can also spread viruses to PCs with which they are connected (Foote 2012 rev 2013).

Online gaming—Although online gaming is typically associated with fun and leisure, cybercriminals take advantage of that mindset daily. A large-scale, sophisticated cyberattack on an online gaming community can have huge implications. The cyberattack on the *Sony PlayStation Network* in 2011 compromised the personal data of more than 77 million users of the service by exposing their personal and financial information (Ben Quinn 2011). Gamers who engage in massively multiplayer online role-playing games such as *World of Warcraft, Guild Wars 2*, and *Final Fantasy XIV*, and social networking games via Facebook have several common threats to watch out for, including gold keylogging, phishing, and gaming bots.

Advance social engineering—All social engineering techniques are based on specific attributes of human decision making known as cognitive biases. These biases are exploited in various combinations to create attack techniques such as pretexting, diversion theft, phishing, baiting, quid pro quo, and tailgating (Crank 2014).

Rise of the project economy/fall of the corporation—Work is being reduced into smaller pieces, changing the process both for companies that buy work and for professionals delivering work for pay. Whether it is outsourcing a function, engaging a consultant or consulting firm, or using freelancers, retired employees, and even crowdsourcing, companies just do not need as many employees as they did 5 years ago. The new workforce model today includes a percentage of the workforce composed of consultants, contractors, and freelancers. Many companies consider as much as half of their workforce as "nonemployees." This brings with it a rise in the use of public cloud-based collaboration services. Technology advances also enabled workers to be remote: working from home, plugging in at Starbucks, and even subcontracting freelancers from overseas. All are cybersecurity challenges.

Advanced persistent threats/hactivism/nation-state cyberterrorism— "The term APT is being commonly used to refer to cyber threats, in particular that of Internet-enabled espionage using a variety of intelligence gathering techniques to access sensitive information, but applies equally to other threats such as that of traditional espionage or attack" (Sophos Inc. 2014). These processes usually target organizations or nations for business or political motives and require a high degree of covertness over a long period. Sophisticated malware is often used to exploit vulnerabilities in systems, and persistence of these attacks the existence of an external command and control process that is continuously monitoring and extracting data from a specific target. APT usually refers to a group, such as a government, with both the capability and the intent to persistently and effectively target a specific entity.

Multitenancy security/threat vector inheritance—Expanded use of hypervisors and multitenant environments adds additional security challenges. Vulnerabilities present in another user's application now represent an unknown threat to your security posture. Bad actors could conceivably use specialized malware to tunnel through virtualization layers in order to attack neighboring systems.

Sector-specific IT security control points (i.e., FedRAMP)—As part of the US Federal Government's "Cloud First" policy, all federally approved CSPs must adhere to security policies and procedures mandated by the Federal Risk and Authorization Management Program (FedRAMP). This US federal government specific requirement dictates automated monitoring of, and reporting on, specified cloud infrastructure security control points. Its success could lead to similar security mandates within government-regulated industries or ones that are deemed critical to national security.

Federated identity, authorization, and access management—Organizations of any significant size will likely procure services from more than one CSP. Implementation of single sign-on processes across multiple providers will inevitably drive an increased need for federated identity, authorization, and access management. Cybersecurity professionals will be called upon to evaluate, deploy, operate, and modify these systems as business models and processes evolve.

Blended personal/corporate IT security—As society continues to move toward blended personal and professional identities in the digital world, professional identities will also continue to be blended with corporate ones. Security professional will be charged with managing an ever-changing tapestry of internal, external, and virtual organizations, roles, and identities.

Security-as-a-Service—"Security as a Service (Secaas) is the next generation of managed security services dedicated to the delivery, over the Internet, of specialized information-security services" (Information Systems Audit and Control Association 2013). While the "low cost, technically acceptable" acquisition model in this area brings its own set of concerns, normal vendor service procurement churn will also increase the cybersecurity team's breadth of responsibility.

Cyber cartels—Harmful results posed by advanced persistent threats can be extraordinary and are rapidly increasing in scale. In fact, cyber cartels will soon surpass drug cartels in posing the largest threat to global security. Companies that are particularly in danger of industrial espionage include producers of high-tech products and those with large research and development divisions (Deloitte Center for Security & Privacy Solutions 2011).

10.9 NATIONAL CYBERSECURITY WORKFORCE FRAMEWORK

In order to address the current training and education challenges, the National Initiative for Cybersecurity Education (NICE) has developed the National Cybersecurity Workforce Framework ("the Framework"). This initiative provides a common lexicon for cybersecurity work. By standardizing terms, the Framework is designed to enhance the education, recruiting, training, development, and retention of a highly qualified workforce.

The Framework uses "Categories" and "Specialty Areas" to group similar types of work. Categories provide an overarching structure for specialty areas groupings, which address typical tasks and skill sets. This framework is intended to describe cybersecurity work independent of organizational structures, job titles, or local conventions. Within any given organization, groups can be organized into positions, career fields, or work roles.

The Categories and specialty areas are shown in Table 10.1.

10.10 UNITED STATES NICE

The US NICE is a national initiative to address cybersecurity education and workforce development. As a public–private partnership between government, academia, and the private sector, it is designed to facilitate change and innovation across the cybersecurity profession. IT's strategic goals are as follows:

- Goal 1: Accelerate Learning and Skills Development

  - Stimulate approaches and techniques that can more rapidly increase the supply of qualified cybersecurity workers

  - Reduce the time and cost for obtaining knowledge, skills, and abilities for in demand work roles

  - Influence employers to shape job descriptions to reflect knowledge, skills, and abilities appropriate for tasks to be performed

  - Pursue displaced workers or underemployed individuals who are available and motivated

  - Identify and fill gaps in cybersecurity skills training to support identified workforce needs

- Goal 2: Nurture a Diverse Learning Community

  - Strengthen formal education programs, cocurricular experiences, training and certifications, and employer-based training

  - Explore tools and techniques that effectively measure and validate knowledge, skills, and abilities

  - Inspire cybersecurity career awareness, exploration, and preparedness with students in elementary and secondary schools

  - Encourage creative and effective efforts to increase the number of underrepresented populations

  - Build on institutional initiatives to improve student success by establishing academic pathways for cybersecurity careers

- Goal 3: Guide Career Development and Workforce Planning

  - Identify and analyze data sources that project present and future workforce demand and supply of qualified cybersecurity workers

  - Promote the National Cybersecurity Workforce Framework and encourage sector implementations

  - Facilitate state and local consortium that identify cyber pathways that address local and national workforce needs

  - Promote tools that assist human resource professionals and hiring managers with recruitment, hiring, promotion, and retention

TABLE 10.1 Cybersecurity Education Categories

Category	Specialty Area Title and Definition
Securely Provision—Specialty areas responsible for conceptualizing, designing, and building secure IT systems, with responsibility for some aspect of the systems' development.	Secure Acquisition—Manages and supports the acquisition life cycle, including planning, determining specifications, selecting, and procuring information and communications technology (ICT) and cybersecurity products used in the organization's design, development, and maintenance of its infrastructure to minimize potential risks and vulnerabilities.
	Secure Software Engineering—Develops, modifies, enhances, and sustains new or existing computer applications, software, or utility programs following software assurance best practices throughout the software life cycle.
	Systems Security Architecture—Designs and develops system concepts and works on the capabilities phases of the systems development life cycle. Translates technology and environmental conditions (e.g., laws, regulations, best practices) into system and security designs and processes.
	Technology Research and Development—Conducts technology and feasibility assessments. Provides, builds, and supports a prototype capability and evaluates its security and utility. Facilitates innovation.
	Systems Requirements Planning—Consults with stakeholders to guide, gather, and evaluate functional and security requirements. Translates these requirements into guidance to stakeholders about the applicability of information systems to meet their needs.
	Test and Evaluation—Develops and conducts processes and procedures (e.g., testing) to evaluate compliance with security requirements.
	Systems Development—Develops technical security solutions to meet the defined requirements.

(Continued)

TABLE 10.1 (CONTINUED) Cybersecurity Education Categories

Category	Specialty Area Title and Definition
Operate and Maintain—Specialty areas responsible for providing the support, administration, and maintenance necessary to ensure effective and efficient IT system performance and security.	Data Administration—Develops, maintains, and administers databases or data management systems that allow for the secure storage, query, and utilization of data. Conducts data integration, data modeling, analytics modeling, and data mining. Customer Service and Technical Support—Provides end users tiered-level customer support by coordinating software, hardware, network, and security issue resolution. May install, configure, troubleshoot, and provide maintenance and training. Network Services—Installs, configures, tests, operates, maintains, and manages network devices including hardware, software, and operating systems that permit information sharing across the full spectrum of transmission using all media. Supports the security of information and information systems. System Administration—Installs, configures, troubleshoots, and maintains server and systems configurations (hardware and software) to ensure their confidentiality, integrity, and availability. Administers server-based systems, security devices, distributed applications, network storage, messaging, and performs systems monitoring. Consults on network, application, and customer service issues to support computer systems' security and sustainability. Systems Security Analysis—Conducts and documents the systems integration, testing, operations, maintenance, and security of an information environment. Coordinates threat and mitigation strategies across the enterprise.
Protect and Defend—Specialty areas responsible for identifying, analyzing, and mitigating threats to internal IT systems or networks.	Enterprise Network Defense (END) Analysis—Uses defensive measures and information collected from a variety of sources to identify, analyze, and report events that occur or might occur within the enterprise network in order to protect information, information systems, and networks from threats.

(Continued)

TABLE 10.1 (CONTINUED) Cybersecurity Education Categories

Category	Specialty Area Title and Definition
	Incident Response—Responds to disruptions within the pertinent domain to mitigate immediate and potential threats. Uses mitigation, preparedness, and response and recovery approaches to maximize survival of life, preservation of property, and information security. Investigates and analyzes relevant response activities and evaluates the effectiveness of and improvements to existing practices.
	Enterprise Network Defense (END) Infrastructure Support—Tests, implements, deploys, maintains, reviews, and administers the infrastructure hardware, software, and documentation that are required to effectively manage network defense resources. Monitors the network to actively remediate unauthorized activities.
	Vulnerability Assessment and Management—Conducts threat and vulnerability assessments and determines deviations from acceptable configurations or policies. Assesses the level of risk and develops and recommends appropriate mitigation countermeasures in operational and nonoperational situations.
Investigate—Specialty areas responsible for investigating cyber events or crimes related to IT systems, networks, and digital evidence.	Digital Forensics—Collects, processes, preserves, analyzes, and presents digital-related evidence to support network vulnerability mitigation and civil, workplace, counterintelligence, or law enforcement (e.g., criminal, fraud) investigations.
	Cyber Investigation—Applies tactics, techniques, and procedures to a full range of tools and processes related to administrative, criminal, and counterintelligence gathering (e.g., in-depth case analyses, continuous monitoring, malware analysis, clear documentation).
Oversee and Govern—Specialty areas responsible for providing leadership, management, direction, or development and advocacy so that the organization may effectively conduct cybersecurity work.	Legal Advice and Advocacy—Provides legal advice and recommendations to leadership and staff on relevant topics within the pertinent subject domain. Advocates legal and policy changes, and makes a case on behalf of the client via written and oral work products, including legal briefs and proceedings.

(Continued)

TABLE 10.1 (CONTINUED) Cybersecurity Education Categories

Category	Specialty Area Title and Definition
	Strategic Planning and Policy Development—Applies technical and organizational knowledge to define an entity's strategic direction, determine resource allocations, establish priorities, and identify programs or infrastructure required to achieve desired goals. Develops policy or advocates for policy change that will support new initiatives or required changes and enhancements.
	Training, Education, and Awareness (TEA)—Develops, plans, coordinates, delivers, and evaluates instructional cybersecurity content using various formats, techniques, and venues.
	Information Systems Security Operations—Oversees and ensures that the appropriate operational security posture (e.g., network and system security, physical and environmental protection, personnel security, incident handling, security training, and awareness) is implemented and maintained for an information system or program. Advises the Authorizing Official (AO), an information system owner, or the Chief Information Security Officer (CISO) on the security of an information system or program.
	Security Program Management—Oversees and manages information security program implementation within the organization or other area of responsibility. Manages strategy, personnel, infrastructure, policy enforcement, emergency planning, security awareness, and other resources.
	Risk Management—Oversees, evaluates, and supports the documentation, validation, and accreditation processes necessary to ensure that new and existing IT systems meet the organization's information assurance and security requirements. Ensures appropriate treatment of risk, compliance, and monitoring assurance from internal and external perspectives.
	Knowledge Management—Manages and administers integrated methods, enabling the organization to identify, capture, catalog, classify, retrieve, and share intellectual capital and information content. The methods may include utilizing processes and tools (e.g., databases, documents, policies, procedures) and expertise pertaining to the organization.

(Continued)

TABLE 10.1 (CONTINUED) Cybersecurity Education Categories

Category	Specialty Area Title and Definition
Collect and Operate—Specialty areas responsible for specialized denial and deception operations and collection of cybersecurity information that may be used to develop intelligence.	Collection Operations—Executes collection using appropriate strategies within the priorities established through the collection management process. Cyber Operations—Performs activities to gather evidence on criminal or foreign intelligence entities in order to mitigate possible or real-time threats; to protect against espionage or insider threats, foreign sabotage, and international terrorist activities; or to support other intelligence activities. Cyber Operations Planning—Performs in-depth joint targeting and cyber planning process. Gathers information and develops detailed operational plans and orders supporting requirements. Conducts strategic and operational-level planning across the full range of operations for integrated information and cyberspace operations.
Analyze—Specialty areas responsible for highly specialized review and evaluation of incoming cybersecurity information to determine its usefulness for intelligence.	All-Source Intelligence—Analyzes threat information from multiple sources, disciplines, and agencies across the Intelligence Community. Synthesizes and places intelligence information in context and draws insights about the possible implications. Exploitation Analysis—Analyzes collected information to identify vulnerabilities and potential for exploitation. Targets—Applies current knowledge of one or more regions, countries, non-state entities, and technologies. Threat Analysis—Identifies and assesses the capabilities and activities of cyber criminals or foreign intelligence entities. Produces findings to help initialize or support law enforcement and counterintelligence investigations or activities.

- Explore international approaches that could inform practice in the United States and share NICE successes with other countries

NICE also encompasses cyber education, research, and workforce components:

- Formal Cybersecurity Education Component—Bolster formal cybersecurity education programs encompassing kindergarten through 12th grade, higher education, and vocational programs, with a focus on the science, technology, engineering, and math disciplines to provide a pipeline of skilled workers for the private sector and government.

- Research—The development of cybersecurity researchers, cybersecurity professionals, cybersecurity-capable workforce, and cybersecurity-aware citizens. A cybersecurity-capable workforce includes not only those who enter computer science, information assurance, IT, and information security fields but also all students and workers affected by cybersecurity issues. A digitally literate workforce that uses technology in a secure manner is imperative to the nation's economy and the security of our critical infrastructure. Just as we teach science, technology, engineering, mathematics, reading, writing, and other critical subjects to all students, we also need to educate all students to use technology securely in order to prepare them for the digital world in which we live.

- Cybersecurity Workforce Component—Cultivating an integrated cybersecurity workforce that is globally competitive from hire to retire, with the knowledge, skills, and ability to protect our nation from existing and emerging challenges.

The NICE initiative also includes the following:

- The Department of Defense (DoD) Cyber Strategy—Intended to guide the development of DoD's cyber forces and strengthen the cyber defense and cyber deterrence posture. It focuses on building cyber capabilities and organizations for DoD's three cyber missions: to defend DoD networks, systems, and information; defend the US homeland and US national interests against cyberattacks of significant consequence; and support operational and contingency plans (April 2015).

- Special Cybersecurity Workforce Project—The US Office of Personnel Management (OPM) is collaborating with the White House Office of Science and Technology Policy, the Chief Human Capital Officers Council (CHCOC), and the Chief Information Officers Council (CIOC) in implementing a special workforce project that tasks federal agencies' cybersecurity, IT, and HR communities to build a statistical data set of existing and future cybersecurity positions in the OPM Enterprise Human Resources Integration (EHRI) data warehouse by the end of FY 2014 (July 2013).

- National Academies of Science Study—*Professionalizing the Nation's Cybersecurity Workforce: Criteria for Decision-Making* considers approaches to increasing the professionalization of the nation's cybersecurity workforce (September 18, 2013).

- Department of Labor (DOL)–sponsored industry competency models—The DOL Cybersecurity Industry Model defines the latest skill and knowledge requirements needed by individuals whose activities affect the security of their organization's cyberspace. The model incorporates competencies identified in the NICE National Cybersecurity Workforce Framework and complements the Framework by including both the competencies needed by the average worker who uses the Internet or the organization's computer network, as well as cybersecurity professionals.

- O*NET OnLine—A tool for career exploration and job analysis! O*NET OnLine has detailed descriptions of the world of work for use by job seekers, workforce development and HR professionals, students, and researchers.

REFERENCES

A. Ben Aissa, R. A. (2010). Quantifying security threats and their potential impacts: A case study. *Innovation in Systems and Software Engineering: A NASA Journal*, 269–281.

Ben Quinn, C. A. (2011). *PlayStation Network hackers access data of 77 million users*. Retrieved from The Guardian: http://www.theguardian.com/technology /2011/apr/26/playstation-network-hackers-data.

Boehme, R. N. (2008). Boehme, R., Nowey, T. In E. F. Irene, *Dependability Metrics* (pp. 176–187).

Business Software Alliance. (2013). *2013 BSA Global Cloud Computing Scorecard*. Washington, DC: Business Software Alliance.

Cloud Security Alliance. (2013). *The Notorious Nine: Cloud Computing Top Threats in 2013*. Cloud Security Alliance. Retrieved from https://downloads .cloudsecurityalliance.org/initiatives/top_threats/The_Notorious_Nine _Cloud_Computing_Top_Threats_in_2013.pdf.

Crank, C. (2014). *Social engineering: How it's used to gain cyber information*. Retrieved from www.scmagazine.com: http://www.scmagazine.com/social -engineering-how-its-used-to-gain-cyber-information/article/358339/.

Deloitte Center for Security & Privacy Solutions. (2011). *Cyber Espionage: The harsh reality of advanced security threats*. London: Deloitte Development, LLC. Retrieved from http://www.deloitte.com/assets/Dcom-UnitedStates /Local%20Assets/Documents/AERS/us_aers_cyber_espionage_07292011 .pdf.

Foote, P. R. (2012 rev 2013). *Cyber Threats to Mobile Phones*. United States Computer Emergency Readiness Team. Pittsburgh, PA: Carnegie Mellon University.

Information Systems Audit and Control Association (ISACA). (2013). *Security as a Service Business Benefits*. Retrieved from www.isaca.org: http://www .isaca.org/Knowledge-Center/Research/Documents/Security-as-a-Service _whp_eng_1213.pdf.

Kimberly Harris-Ferrante, D. C. (2014). *Industries Aim to Evolve Cloud Computing Beyond Support Functions to More Strategic Uses*. Retrieved from Gartner .com: https://www.gartner.com/doc/2027216.

Latifa Ben Arfa Rabaia, M. J. (2014). *A cybersecurity model in cloud computing environments*. Retrieved from Journal of King Saud University—Computer and Information Sciences (Volume 25, Issue 1, January 2013, Pages 63–75): http://www.sciencedirect.com/science/article/pii/S131915781200033X.

Mayer, N. (2009). *Model-Based Management of Information System Security Risk*.

National Institute of Standards and Technologies. (2013). *Improving Critical Infrastructure Cybersecurity, Executive Order 13636, Preliminary Cybersecurity Framework*. Gaithersburg, MD: National Institute of Standards and Technologies.

Sophos Inc. (2014, June 26). *APT – Advanced Persistent Threats – Part 1: Definition*. Retrieved from http://itsecformanagers.com: http://itsecformanagers .com/2014/06/26/apt-advanced-persistent-threats-part-1-definition/.

The Open Group: Jericho Forum. (2009). *Cloud Cube Model: Selecting Cloud Formations for Secure Collaboration*. Jericho Forum. Retrieved from https:// collaboration.opengroup.org/jericho/cloud_cube_model_v1.0.pdf.

Tsiakis, T. (2010). Information security expenditures: A techno-economic analysis. *International Journal of Computer Science and Network Security (IJCSNS)*, 7–11.

Weinman, J. (2012). *Cloudonomics: The Business Value of Cloud Computing*. Hoboken, NJ: John Wiley & Sons.

Wendy Currie, J. S. (2014). A Cross-Country Study of Cloud Computing. *Twenty Second European Conference on Information Systems*, (p. 14). Tel Aviv. Retrieved from http://ecis2014.eu/E-poster/files/0247-file1.pdf.

Zhang, X. W. (2010). Information security risk management framework for the cloud computing environments. *10th International Conference on Computer and Information Technology (CIT)*, 1328–1334.

CHAPTER 11

Next-Generation Business Models and Strategies

ENTERPRISES ARE APPLYING CLOUD to generate additional revenue streams by enhancing, extending, and inventing new customer value propositions, and cloud is being used to improve, transform, and create new organization and industry value chains. This has resulted in shifts in who creates value, as well as how it is created, delivered, and captured (Berman et al. 2012).

11.1 STRATEGIC REINVENTION

- Reinvent customer relationships
- Innovate product/services rapidly
- Build new/improved business models

11.1.1 Customer Value Propositions

- Enhance: Organizations can use cloud to improve current products and services and enhance customers' experiences to retain current and attract new customers, garnering incremental revenue.

- Extend: Cloud can help a company create new products and services or utilize new channels or payment methods to attract existing or adjacent customer segments in an attempt to generate significant new revenues.

- Invent: Companies can use cloud to create a new "need" and own a new market, attracting new customer segments and generating entirely new revenue streams.

11.1.2 Value Chains

- Improve: Cloud adoption can help an organization maintain its place in an existing value chain through increased efficiency and an improved ability to partner, source, and collaborate.

- Transform: By assisting in developing new operating capabilities, cloud can help a company change its role within its industry or enter a different industry.

- Create: Organizations can use cloud to build a new industry value chain or disintermediate an existing one, radically changing industry economics.

11.2 BETTER DECISIONS

- Use analytics extensively to derive insights from big data

- Share data seamlessly across applications

- Make data-driven, evidence-based decisions

Video Lecture: Business Analytics Strategies (https://oncloud.talentlms .com/unit/view/id:2469)

11.3 DEEPER COLLABORATION

- Make it easier to locate and leverage knowledge of experts anywhere in the ecosystem

- Improve integration between development and operations

- Collaborate across organization and ecosystem

REFERENCE

Berman, S., Kesterson-Townes, L., Marshall, A., Srivathsa, R. (2012). *The Power of Cloud*. IBM Institute for Business Value executive report. IBM Global Services, Somers, New York. Retrieved from https://www.ibm.com/cloud-computing/us/en/assets/power-of-cloud-for-bus-model-innovation.pdf.

Appendix A: OnCloud Training Security Offerings

Access requires registration with OnCloud Training at http://www.oncloud training.com.

- Critical Threats (https://oncloud.talentlms.com/unit/view/id:1817)
- Cloud Computing Threat Vectors (https://oncloud.talentlms.com/unit /view/id:1818)
- Cloud Computing Risk Management (https://oncloud.talentlms.com /unit/view/id:1819)
- Intrusion Detection Public Infrastructure (https://oncloud.talentlms .com/unit/view/id:1820)
- Cloud Forensics Defined (https://oncloud.talentlms.com/unit/view /id:1936)
- Security and Privacy (https://oncloud.talentlms.com/unit/view/id:1937)
- eDiscovery in the Cloud (https://oncloud.talentlms.com/unit/view /id:1938)
- Digital Forensics (https://oncloud.talentlms.com/unit/view/id:1939)
- Critical Aspects of Cloud Forensics (https://oncloud.talentlms.com /unit/view/id:1940)
- Cloud Forensics Challenges and Opportunities (https://oncloud.talent lms.com/unit/view/id:1941)

- What is FedRAMP (https://oncloud.talentlms.com/unit/view/id:1827)

- FedRAMP for 3PAOs (https://oncloud.talentlms.com/unit/view/id:1824)

- FedRAMP for CSPs (https://oncloud.talentlms.com/unit/view/id:1825)

- FedRAMP for Federal Agencies (https://oncloud.talentlms.com/unit/view/id:1826)

Appendix B: Relevant Articles and Publications

Excerpt from Kevin L. Jackson's IEEE article

IEEE GovCloud: Making a Difference for Global Governments

INTRODUCTION

On February 8, 2011, then US Chief Information Officer (CIO) Vivek Kundra released the US Federal Cloud Computing Strategy.* In the executive summary, he laid out the sad state of affairs that was the US Federal Government's IT environment:

> The Federal Government's current Information Technology (IT) environment is characterized by low asset utilization, a fragmented demand for resources, duplicative systems, environments which are difficult to manage, and long procurement lead times. These inefficiencies negatively impact the Federal Government's ability to serve the American public.
>
> Cloud Computing has the potential to play a major part in addressing these inefficiencies and improving government service delivery. The Cloud Computing model can significantly help agencies grappling with the need to provide highly reliable, innovative services quickly despite resource constraints.

These words heralded the start of the US Federal Government's Cloud First policy. It also turned out to be the start of a global trend toward the

---

* https://www.whitehouse.gov/sites/default/files/omb/assets/egov_docs/federal-cloud-computing -strategy.pdf

adoption of Cloud Computing services by governments around the world. Some of the more well-known initiatives include the following:

- European Commission (EC) commitment* to Cloud Computing and a long-term plan for propagating a common set of rules aimed at fostering a cohesive market structure among the European Union member states for cloud service providers.

- Japan's "Smart Cloud Strategy"[†] sets forth a high-level plan to "maximize the use of cloud services," "promote the widespread use of ICT," and "amass and share a wealth of information and knowledge beyond the boundaries of companies and industries across the entire social system" with an eye toward creating "new economic growth" and "bolstering Japan's international competitiveness."

- The United Kingdom G-Cloud strategy[‡] that envisions the government developing a policy around governmental use of Cloud Computing, followed by a widespread initiative to replace and supplement legacy software systems with multitenant, shared Cloud Computing services.

Cloud Computing's global financial impact is also impressive. In November 2014, an International Data Corporation report[§] predicted that the value of public IT cloud services spending will reach $56.6 billion in 2014 and grow to more than $127 billion in 2018. This represents a 5-year compound annual growth rate (CAGR) of 22.8%, which is approximately six times the rate for the overall IT market. By 2018, public IT cloud services are expected to account for more than half of worldwide software, server, and storage spending growth.

---

* http://ec.europa.eu/digital-agenda/en/european-cloud-computing-strategy

[†] http://www.soumu.go.jp/main_sosiki/joho_tsusin/eng/councilreport/pdf/100517_1.pdf

[‡] https://www.gov.uk/government/uploads/system/uploads/attachment_data/file/266214/government-cloud-strategy_0.pdf

[§] https://www.idc.com/getdoc.jsp?containerId=251730

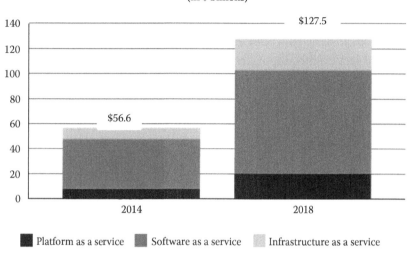

Worldwide public IT cloud services spending by segment
(in $ billions)

$127.5

$56.6

2014   2018

■ Platform as a service   ■ Software as a service   Infrastructure as a service

IDC defines "public sector" as that part of the economy and the organizations concerned with providing basic government services. While the composition of this defined segment varies by country, it typically covers services such as public safety/emergency response, defense, transportation infrastructure and services, primary education, social services, and services that facilitate income equity.

The research firm also identified key market drivers that affect public sector technology investment, management, and evaluation, namely:

- **Operational efficiency.** Moving from narrower-focused IT cost reduction to broader overall strategies that will reduce operational costs, which includes business process reengineering and shared services

- **Digital engagement strategy.** Rationalizing and pervasively investing in IT devices and solutions that effectively enable the conduct of government business

- **Mission effectiveness.** Moving from measuring program outcomes to measuring mission outcomes

- **Economic sustainability.** The desire to implement citizen-facing programs and services through strategies that foster regional quality of life and economic growth/competitiveness

Since Cloud Computing can provide a path toward enhanced utility of information technology at reduced cost and all the public sector goals fall squarely within IEEE mission of *Advancing Technology for Humanity*, IEEE GovCloud is truly poised to deliver true value to IEEE's many members that service this important industry vertical.

GOVERNMENTAL CLOUD COMPUTING ROLES

One of the findings from World Trade Institute government cloud strategies* is that governments have taken on several different roles with respect to their approaches to Cloud Computing. Although these categories have overlapping characteristics, they can be analytically distinguished among six basic roles:

- Governments as Users—adopting Cloud Computing services to take advantage of its costs savings and innovative features. Governments are replacing their legacy IT systems with Cloud Computing technologies and implementing new cloud-based tools for collaboration and information sharing. In meeting their mission requirements, the public sector is essentially using cloud the same way that consumers do.

- Governments as Regulators—acting through legislative, judicial, and regulatory branches to implement policy through the rule of law. This activity is typically issues driven and does not follow a "strategy," "blueprint," or plan.

- Governments as Coordinators—coordinate public and private initiatives, through standard setting processes, and the sharing of information between private and public stakeholders. Governments are playing and will continue to play a powerful role in convening stakeholders, developing collaborative solutions, and pursuing consensus between companies, governmental agencies, international organizations, and other Cloud Computing industry actors.

- Governments as Promoters—actively promoting the cloud industry by endorsement, funding, and incubation programs. Governments seek to encourage the growth of national or regional private Cloud Computing industry and its technologies.

* http://www.wti.org/fileadmin/user_upload/nccr-trade.ch/wp3/WP_Government_and_Cloud _Computing_083013.pdf

- Governments as Researchers—conducting and funding research on technical or societal issues related to Cloud Computing. In determining the best courses of action for its many constituents, governments do research that focuses on finding answers to key questions about the economic and societal effects of cloud.

- Governments as Service Providers—providing cloud services for use by other government agencies or the public. In this role, governmental organizations must also avoid excessive competition with the same private providers that they are trying to promote.

In order to structure and organize IEEE GovCloud selection and publication of government Cloud Computing articles, we will adopt this classification of governmental roles with a goal of providing both broad and relevant industry coverage. We will also strive to provide linkage to the four primary market drivers listed earlier.

GLOBAL GOVERNMENT CLOUD TRANSITION EXAMPLES

Some examples of how governments around the world are jumping into Cloud Computing include the following:

California State Resources Agency*

California State Resources Agency (CNRA) is responsible for managing natural resources that spans 150,000+ square miles and 38 million people. Composed of more than 29 organizations, this US state agency provides the real-time information needed to make important decisions and respond quickly to natural disasters. In the past, CNRA's systems took up to a month to load critical data. This drove CNRA to consider other business models and resulted in the deployment of a new private cloud infrastructure. The results of this transition to cloud included

- 35% cost reduction across 29 agencies

- 300% increase in available storage space

- 30% decrease in storage footprint

---

* http://community.netapp.com/t5/Company/State-of-California-A-Model-for-Government-Cloud-Computing/ba-p/84663

Australian Maritime Safety Authority*

In 2009, the Australian Maritime Safety Authority (AMSA) developed a cloud-based application tool to track the compliance of international ships to safety standards across 14 geographically separated ports. This cloud-based approach enabled AMSA to

- Acquire a solution that was significantly cheaper and faster to deploy compared to noncloud solutions

- Increase user satisfaction through improved functionality and remote access on mobile devices

- Accelerate organizational learning and maturity in using and procuring cloud services

Estonia eGovernment†

After passing the Digital Signatures in 2000, the state standardized on national public key infrastructure that bound citizen identities to individual cryptographic keys. That foundational law forced all decentralized government systems to become digital as citizens opted for convenience. The national identification card–embedded digital chip carried two certificates: one for full legal signatures and a second for authenticating to any trusting website or service (used widely from government services to Internet banks). Through this cloud-based system:

- More than 1.3 million Estonians have authenticated 230 million times and given 140 million legally binding signatures.

- Estonia became the first country in the world to allow voting for local elections. The system was also used for both Estonian and European Parliament Elections. Citizens were able to vote from wherever they physically were, resulting in votes from 105 separate countries.

- Tax deductions on mortgages come directly from data interchange with commercial banks.

- Health records and prescriptions are now fully digitized.

---

* http://www.finance.gov.au/sites/default/files/australian-government-cloud-computing-policy-3 .pdf

† http://www.bhorowitz.com/estonia_the_little_country_that_cloud

Singapore Smart City*

Singapore is driving the pursuit of a cloud environment in order to leverage the benefits of increased business agility, higher levels of system resilience, and the optimized use of computing resources. The overall cloud strategy deploys the appropriate cloud for the appropriate need by adopting a multipronged approach. The nation intends to

- Leverage commercially available public cloud offerings where appropriate in order to benefit from its lower cost
- Implement a private government cloud for whole-of-government use where security and governance requirements cannot be met by public clouds
- Enable interoperability within the whole-of-government cloud

As part of the "Smart Nation" vision, the city-state uses cloud to enable

- Driverless buggies in Jurong
- Smart Elderly Monitoring and Alert System
- Citizen Connect Centers with officers to help citizens access government services
- Citizen services such as IRAS' e-filing, MHA's Passport Application Services, and NLB book borrowing

GovCloud TRANSITION GUIDANCE

For those IT professionals supporting this global Cloud Computing adoption trend, a KPMG study entitled "Exploring the Cloud: A Global Study of Governments' Adoption of Cloud"† provides some insight into past lessons learned. Organized based on the roles played by the participants, specific guidance for enabling this important transition include the following:

---

* http://www.pmo.gov.sg/mediacentre/transcript-prime-minister-lee-hsien-loongs-speech-smart
  -nation-launch-24-november
† https://www.kpmg.com/ES/es/ActualidadyNovedades/ArticulosyPublicaciones/Documents
  /Exploring-the-Cloud.pdf

For Government Leaders

- Identify gaps in your processes and determine if and how cloud can help fill those gaps.

- Evaluate collaboration and information exchange needs with providers, constituents and stakeholders, and other agencies.

- Assess the economics and risk profile of a private versus public cloud and actively manage security risks.

- Estimate risks versus potential rewards using tools such as cost–benefit and return-on-investment analysis.

- Understand where the cloud provider—internal or external—will force organizational process changes, assess the change management implications, and plan.

- Validate Cloud Computing cost-savings claims for your organization and test them against total cost of ownership, including the cost of compliance and related change management implications.

- Test the customization needs of your agency. The more customization required, the less likelihood of cloud success.

- Identify business integration issues in your entity, with specific emphasis on data that are now scattered across the enterprise.

- Assess internal staff, current roles and responsibilities, change management needed, and how well current skills map to the cloud model.

- Consider where a cloud program fits within the existing capital budgeting and approval process. You must pay particular attention to the existing IT governance models.

- Determine how operating continuity and disaster recovery will factor into your cloud migration strategy.

- Understand the contracting process and the degree of flexibility needed from both your organization and the provider.

- Consider service level agreements and how they will be managed.

- Assess your vendor management risk strategy in the context of current and future cloud technology.

- Determine assurance reporting needs you will require from your cloud vendor. What worked for outsourcing may not provide the assurance you need in a cloud environment.

- Ensure that all regulatory requirements are met in the commingled world of cloud, internal audit, global security, and data privacy.

For Government IT Professionals

- Develop a comprehensive cloud strategy and plan of action. Create the enterprise vision and roadmap for cloud and identify proof-of-concept opportunities.

- Assess whether your technology platforms are an accelerator or inhibitor to your corporate strategy.

- Educate relevant executives on cloud's realistic capabilities and potential.

- Deploy competent specialists to study the cloud market, its capabilities, offerings, and providers.

- Evaluate the interoperability of cloud solutions against current applications, platforms, and infrastructure. Objectively assess their readiness for cloud migration.

- Redefine the role of the CIO as it evolves from IT provider to chief integration officer, who has the opportunity to drive process models and innovation.

- Align your plans with various scenarios for cloud adoption and deployment across each cloud layer and across different IT and business operating areas.

- Interpret cloud services and capabilities planning in the context of your third-party provider contracts.

- Design, develop, and deploy operating governance and risk management programs from the IT perspective of Cloud Computing services.

For Agency Professionals and Process Owners

- Work closely with IT leadership to develop a comprehensive cloud strategy and plan of action.

- Focus on the process value and potential of cloud over its technical capabilities or merits. Avoid the creation of disparate data sets.

- Develop policies and checks to ensure that all groups implement cloud-based processes in close collaboration with IT.

- Assess the implications of deploying applications that are more standardized and less customizable.

- Benchmark cloud usage among other agencies and across private enterprise. Assess opportunities for improvement in core activities, provisioning, or other processes.

For Cloud Service and Technology Providers

- Avoid overpromising. Failures will prove costly.

- Where possible, overdeliver. Positive word of mouth will channel opportunities to established and well-documented providers.

- Be realistic on cost-savings claims and provide examples with applicable documentation. Ensure appropriate performance measures by continually monitoring results.

- Develop contracts and pricing that deliver true flexibility and scalability.

- Educate customers and prospects on the benefits of cloud. Intangible benefits such as optimization, agility, and innovation may require real-world examples. These benefits may not be equally shared between an IT department and frontline government functions.

- Be proactive about communicating the challenges of rapid and multiple cloud investments and deployments.

- Assist in developing an integration roadmap with existing infrastructure and other cloud offers.

- Plan to continually address ongoing integration requirements.

- Address security and data ownership concerns.

- Assist clients in developing new KPIs to measure their investment.

- Optimize your business model in key areas such as customer management, risk and compliance, revenue recognition, and tax structures. Recognize that although a wider international footprint increases complexity, it also tends to expand the potential benefits of a more optimized approach.

For Risk Professionals and Internal Advisory Committees

- Ensure adequately skilled professionals are in place to assess and monitor the risk and controls management aspects of cloud.

- Embed risk and controls consideration in cloud selection processes.

- Understand that traditional IT control protocols may be non-existent in a cloud service provider and that funding, development, and the implementation life cycle may require a new governance model.

- Users have access to public cloud services; thus, policies and safeguards will be necessary to prevent commingling of data and applications.

- Involve risk and internal advisory groups in cloud services planning and vendor selection processes and cloud service operations.

- Evaluate how information will be secured and how privacy and confidentiality will be maintained.

- Determine how Cloud Computing adoption will affect regulatory and compliance requirements.

- Establish a formalized assurance program, whether through internal audit or independent assurance reporting (SOC reports).

- Understand the global, regional, and local implications of the cloud environment. For government groups that regulate or otherwise work with the private sector, this will include an appreciation for evolving tax treatments of cloud environments.

While this approach may seem strange for an organization with such deep technical pedigree, we believe that it will help our readers better address the much tighter linkage between business/mission models and technical implementations that successful Cloud Computing deployments demand. This explicit linkage should also support an IT organization's transition from a supporting cost center to the government business and mission innovation center that today's IT organization must become.

Appendix C: Cloud Computing for the Business of Government

This is an excerpt from Kevin Jackson's book:

GovCloud: Cloud Computing for the Business of Government

Softcover: 232 pages

Publisher: Government Training Inc.

Language: English

ISBN-13: 978-0-9832361-3-9

INTRODUCTION

IT and the Federal Government

Information technology (IT) should enable the government to better serve the American people, but despite spending more than $600 billion on IT over the past decade, the federal government has achieved little of the productivity improvements that the private industry has realized from IT. Too often, federal IT projects run overbudget and behind schedule, or fail to deliver promised functionality. Many projects use "grand design" approaches that aim to deliver functionality every few years, rather than breaking projects into more manageable chunks and demanding new functionality every few quarters. In addition, the federal government too often relies on large, custom, proprietary systems when "light technologies" or shared services exist.

Government officials have been trying to adopt best practices for years—from the Raines Rules of the 1990s through the Clinger–Cohen Act and the acquisition regulations that followed, but obstacles have always gotten in the way. This plan attempts to clear these obstacles, allowing agencies to leverage IT to create a more efficient and effective government.

Over the last 18 months, we have engaged the federal IT, acquisition, and program management communities; industry experts; and academics. We have conducted listening sessions with Congress, agency chief information officers (CIOs), and senior procurement executives. We have received detailed input and recommendations from many industry groups such as TechAmerica. This engagement process has led to recommendations for IT reform in the areas of operational efficiency and large-scale IT program management.

A 25-point action plan is designed to deliver more value to the American taxpayer. These actions have been planned over the next 18 months and place ownership with OMB and agency operational centers, as appropriate. While the 25 points may not solve all federal IT challenges, they will address many of the most pressing, persistent challenges. This plan requires a focus on execution and is designed to establish some early wins to garner momentum for our continued efforts. Active involvement from agency leadership is critical to the success of these reforms. As such, the federal CIO will work with the President's Management Council to successfully implement this plan.

Some highlights of the implementation plan include the following:

- Turnaround or terminate at least one-third of underperforming projects in the IT portfolio within the next 18 months.

- Shift to "Cloud First" policy. Each agency will identify three "must move" services within 3 months, and move one of those services to the cloud within 12 months and the remaining two within 18 months.

- Reduce the number of federal data centers by at least 800 by 2015.

- Only approve funding of major IT programs that

  - Have a dedicated program manager and a fully staffed integrated program team

  - Use a modular approach with usable functionality delivered every 6 months

  - Use specialized IT acquisition professionals

- Work with Congress to

  - Consolidate commodity IT funding under the agency CIOs

  - Develop flexible budget models that align with modular development

- Launch an interactive platform for pre-RFP agency–industry collaboration.

Vivek Kundra
US Chief Information Officer
The White House

A full transcript of the action plan is attached as Appendix D.

US Government IT Today

The US Government is the world's largest consumer of IT, spending more than $76 billion annually on more than 10,000 different systems. Fragmentation of systems, poor project execution, and the drag of legacy technology in the federal government have presented barriers to achieving the productivity and performance gains found when technology is deployed effectively in the private sectors.

"The Obama Administration is changing the way business is done in Washington and bringing a new sense of responsibility to how we manage taxpayer dollars. We are working to bring the spirit of American innovation and the power of technology to improve performance and lower the cost of government operations," said Federal Chief Information Officer Vivek Kundra.

In September 2009, the federal government announced its Cloud Computing Initiative. Cloud Computing has the potential to greatly reduce waste, increase data center efficiency and utilization rates, and lower operating costs. The initiative included details on deployment models, service models, and common characteristics of Cloud Computing.

"As we move to the cloud, we must be vigilant in our efforts to ensure that the standards are in place for a Cloud Computing environment that provides for security of government information, protects the privacy of our citizens, and safeguards our national security interests," Kundra said.

Appendix D: Implementation of Cloud Brokerage

This is an excerpt from Kevin Jackson's book:

GovCloud II: Implementation and Cloud Brokerage Services

Softcover: 165 pages

Publisher: Government Training Inc.

Language: English

ISBN-13: 978-1-937246-41-9

OVERVIEW

Cloud Computing is a new approach in the provisioning and consumption of information technology (IT). While technology is a crucial component, the real value of Cloud Computing lies in its ability to enable new capabilities or in the execution of current capabilities in more efficient and effective ways.

Although the current hype around Cloud Computing has focused on expected cost savings, the true value is really found in the mission and business enhancements these techniques can provide. When properly deployed, the Cloud Computing model provides greatly enhanced mission and business capability without a commensurate increase in resource (time, people, or money) expenditures.

The use of commodity components, coupled with highly automated controls, enables Cloud Computing. These characteristics also enable the economic model that makes it so disruptive to the status quo. As an example, the Software-as-a-Service (SaaS) cloud delivery model typically does not require any advance usage commitment or long-term contractual arrangements. SaaS not only changes the typical software vendor business model but also radically changes the strategy, budgeting, buying, and management options for the buyer. When Salesforce.com proved the viability of SaaS, the software subscription model was instantly endangered as a profitable business model. Amazon Web Services is similarly attacking data center hosting with its Virtual Private Datacenter Infrastructure-as-a-Service (IaaS) offering.

Looking at this phenomenon from another angle, different Cloud Computing deployment models are actually changing what it means to be an IT professional. Since the days of the first computer, IT workers have prided themselves in their ability to design, build, operate, and fix the enterprise hardware and software components that comprise the IT lifeblood of organizations—both in the public and private sectors. These tightly knit teams worked hard to keep these custom-made platforms updated, patched, and ready to meet daily business and mission requirements. In the Cloud Computing world, IT infrastructure that is not delivering differentiating value is viewed as worthless cost. Critical business applications such as e-mail, Customer Resource Management, Human Resource Management, and Enterprise Resource Planning are being routed to more capable cloud providers of these same services. This transition puts the enterprise IT professional into a service management role, responsible for helping his or her internal customers better use externally provided IT services. The new enterprise IT department is more of a service organization than the traditional delivery organization.

The new cloud economic model also radically changes the view of what's actually possible. Traditional IT procurement and provisioning processes have historically driven timelines associated with the delivery or fielding of improved information and data processing capabilities. Multiple threads of development, test, training, and maintenance can also tax an organization's short- and long-term financial resources. IaaS and Platform-as-a-Service options not only can eliminate or limit capital expenditures but also can reduce or eliminate the expectation of operations and sustainment costs. The time required to realize mission or business value is substantially reduced as well. With these differences, the impossible can suddenly become not only possible but often can lead to new mission capabilities or brand-new, cloud-enabled, revenue-generating businesses.

CLOUD COMPUTING CHALLENGES

Despite the myriad benefits of Cloud Computing solutions, several challenges still exist. Being a young industry, there are few tools, procedures, or standard data formats or service interfaces in place to guarantee data, computer application, and service portability. As evidenced with a well-known situation involving the services failure of Amazon's Elastic Compute Cloud, outages can be a potential risk—and can have widespread implications for consumers of cloud services. This risk becomes even more severe if a mission-critical environment could be affected.

A benefit as well as a challenge, security concerns have also slowed the widespread adoption of Cloud Computing. A variety of security concerns exist. According to the article, "Three Cloud Computing Risks to Consider," in *Information Security Magazine* (June 2009), "the logging and auditing controls provided by some [cloud] vendors are not yet as robust as the logging providing within enterprises and enterprise applications," which can put critical and sensitive data and information at risk. Security, of course, becomes increasingly critical in defense and intelligence IT environments.

For the government market, the lack of regulations and compliance standards is also a cause for concern. Currently, no federal regulations are in place to govern Cloud Computing, and according to an April 2011 Information Systems Audit and Control Association survey of 1800 chief information officers (CIOs), compliance is a top risk. Approximately 30% of the CIOs surveyed said that "compliance projects are the biggest driver for IT risk-related projects"—particularly in public clouds. Specific to federal environments, data sovereignty is a challenge. According to a speech given by former federal CIO Vivek Kundra at an April 7, 2010, National Institute of Standards and Technology (NIST) forum, "[Data sovereignty] is not going to be a question of technology. [Data sovereignty] is going to be a question of international law, and treaties that we will need to engage in the coming years." CIO Kundra later added: "We've got a very diverse interpretation and a very diverse perspective when it comes to privacy or international security, if you look at our neighbors—Canada or Mexico—versus what's happening in the European Union."

US GovCloud

The Obama administration has identified Cloud Computing as a means to achieve savings in IT budgets across federal agencies—across the board—and to address various other challenges (e.g., delays to capabilities and other inefficiencies) that have negatively affected IT implementations. In his fiscal year 2011 budget, President Barack Obama ordered a 3-year freeze in spending for non–defense, intelligence, and national security programs and the trimming of the budgets of some federal agencies by 5%. At a July 1, 2010, House subcommittee hearing, CIO Kundra testified: "To do more than less [in terms for federal spending], we need game changing technologies. Cloud Computing is one such technology."

The federal government is in the early stages of a decade-long process to "move to the cloud," but has taken definitive steps in its adoption. Several key milestones have been achieved during the past 2 years in support of this effort:

1. **2009:** Establishment of the General Services Administration (GSA) Cloud Computing Program Office to coordinate the government's Cloud Computing efforts; assembly of a public–private sector Industry Summit to discuss the benefits and risks of Cloud Computing; and creation of Security and Standards Working Groups to encourage collaboration and discussion on Cloud Computing by federal agencies.

2. **2010:** Commencement of the development of federal security certification and accreditation processes for cloud services; convening of a NIST-hosted, public–private sector "Cloud Computing Forum and Workshop" to collaboratively develop cloud standards; release of a 25-point federal IT reform plan; announcement by GSA and Federal Chief Information Officers Council on the requirements for the Federal Risk and Authorization Management Program, a standard approach for the federal government to access and authorize secure Cloud Computing services and products.

	Action item	Owner(s)	Within 6 mos.	6–12 mos.	12–18 mos.
1	Complete detailed implementation plans to consolidate 800 data centers by 2015	OMB, agencies	●		
2	Create a government-wide marketplace for data center availability	OMB, GSA			●
3	Shift to a "cloud first" policy	OMB, agencies	●		
4	Stand-up contract vehicles for secure IaaS solutions	GSA	●		
5	Stand-up contract vehicles for "commodity" services	GSA		●	
6	Develop a strategy for shared services	Federal CIO		●	

3. **2011:** Release of the Federal Cloud Computing Strategy (per the Obama administration's 25-point IT reform plan) and award of 12 GSA IaaS blanket purchase agreements.

Appendix E: The Web Services and Service-Oriented Architecture Revolution—Using Web Services to Deliver

What others are saying about the book...

If you're ready to propel your enterprise into the next technological realm—if you're interested in architecting an enterprise that is agile enough to respond to rapidly changing business drivers—if you're ready for a revolution in traditional approaches to technology innovation, then this book is the light in what has been a somewhat obscure tunnel. Author Melvin Greer gives a timely, insightful, and easy to grasp roadmap for leveraging SOA, and more specifically web services-based SOA, to realize dramatic improvement in interoperability, scalability, flexibility, reusability and the all important cost efficiency.

N. McLean
Lockheed Martin, Washington, DC, USA

A wonderfully concise book without the typically verbose pay-per-word variants the IT book market has too much of! I'll lend my copy to whichever customer needs to know the business value of SOA—AND whoever needs to realize NOW is the time to go ahead!

K. Karre
Nacka, Sweden

This is an excerpt from Melvin Greer's book:

The Web Services and Service Oriented Architecture Revolution: Using Web Services to Deliver Business Value

Hardcover: 108 pages

Publisher: iUniverse, Inc.

Language: English

ISBN-10: 0595676065

ISBN-13: 978-0595676064

THE WEB SERVICES AND *Service Oriented Architecture Revolution* is a business guide to understanding the value of emerging Web-based technologies. This book is designed to give business and technical leaders a practical roadmap in implementing service-oriented architectures. Even the most ardent Web services skeptics should take action now. While the future promises revolutionary benefits such as enterprise transformation, other tangible benefits such as cost reduction, collaborative commerce, and increased agility are achievable today. In the worst-case scenario, if the Web Services Revolution fails to deliver on the long-term vision and value proposition, standards-based integration approaches are already proving enterprise-ready in real-world productive applications. By acting now, enterprises can reap near-term rewards while building a foundation to keep them from being left behind as this emerging technology matures and starts paying even bigger dividends. The bottom line is that enterprises have little to lose and potentially much to gain by following a well-conceived Web services game plan now that gradually and progressively invests in standards-based integration capabilities and service-oriented architectures.

While Web services technology is a straightforward extension of existing Internet technology, its ultimate impact on the business enterprise will be profound. The Web Services Revolution is therefore about providing dramatic business performance improvements through incremental technology innovation. While the initial focus of the revolution is on cost reduction, the ultimate objective is to enable the "Agile Enterprise."

Early Web services hype focused attention on the services discovery aspect of Web services where applications are expected to find each other and automatically collaborate regardless of where each physically exists on the Internet. This promise still faces severe security, trust, service level agreement, and other obstacles that to some have given the whole Web Services Revolution a "pie in the sky" reputation.

This current marketplace disillusionment notwithstanding, the Web Services Revolution provides immediate, real-world business benefits to those willing and able to develop and follow a well-conceived Web services game plan. Creating a plan and embarking on this journey is not an easy endeavor, and the stakes are high, but some business enterprises are already achieving significant benefits in actual mission-critical, high-performance, productive applications that rely on Web services technology.

Thus, the real question is not whether your business enterprise can achieve success through Web services technology. With patience and the right help, your business enterprise can succeed. The more interesting question is whether your business enterprise can afford not to begin the migration to this emerging technology while your competitors do.

THE NEXT LOGICAL PROGRESSION OF THE WEB

Web services technology is an extension of existing Internet technology. For this reason, Web services enjoy certain advantages over proprietary integration technology. One advantage is that Web services protocols encounter fewer problems passing through firewalls than many proprietary communication methods. This can result in reduced implementation costs and can even translate into hardware savings.

For example, some proprietary B2B solutions require a separate instance of the software to be located on servers in the DMZ between an enterprise's inner and outer firewalls. Enterprise information security policies often prevent proprietary protocols from passing through both firewalls without a hop on a B2B server located in the DMZ. This additional server, or multiple servers in cases where high availability through redundancy is required, can be expensive. Since Web services protocols use the HTTP (hypertext transaction protocol) running on TCP/IP, the basic protocol of the Web, secured, authenticated Web services communications typically sail through both firewalls without the need for special firewall configuration or an additional DMZ server for security purposes that is typically required for many proprietary protocols.

As an Internet technology, Web services technology is the next logical progression of the Web. The World Wide Web got its name because the essence of hypertext technology is imbedding links to other locations and other sites within the text of a Web page. Taken as a whole, these hypertext links within each Web page form a Web of linked Internet sites world-wide. Accordingly, the first generation of the Web was about human-to-computer interaction. It was about helping human beings interact with a distributed network of computers in better, more powerful ways. This user friendliness in Generation 1 popularized the Web with masses of people worldwide.

The Internet grew out of the military and academic communities' experiments with distributed computing. As a result, not-for-profit collaboration and knowledge-sharing activities dominated the initial use of the Web. In fact, there was some debate at that time about the legitimacy of using the Internet for commercial purposes. This debate soon became moot as Generation 2 of the Web—Internet Commerce—began in earnest in the mid-1990s.

The Web revolutionized human-to-computer interaction in Generation 1 as it ushered in a momentous change in distributed computing. However, B2B commerce over the Web was still faced with significant challenges in Generation 2 that traditional B2B approaches like EDI never adequately addressed. Since the essence of B2B commerce involves computer-to-computer interaction, the computers involved must speak the same language. In reality, this is rarely the case, and security issues compound the computer-to-computer interoperability problem.

Therefore, by the turn of the century during the second generation of the Web, the intense demand for easier integration among enterprises on diverse platforms stimulated mass support for action. (See revolutionary condition #1.) The resulting movement focused on simplifying computer-to-computer interaction over the Web through effective and widely accepted messaging and data encapsulation standards. XML and Web services emerged as an appealing underlying framework providing direction to the movement (revolutionary condition #2). Standards bodies soon took the responsibility of providing the organizational structure to coordinate the movement (revolutionary condition #3).

Appendix F: Software as a Service Inflection Point—Using Cloud Computing to Achieve Business Agility

What others are saying about the book...

While the myths about Cloud Computing, Software as a Service (SaaS) and the future of application systems keep being spread around by users, vendors, so-called IT gurus and even by the general Internet audience, some people are beginning to sort out through the haystack and to point us in the right direction. Taking a series of myths and translating them to real life terms, products and companies is one of the feats achieved by Melvin Greer in his new book. Whether you are looking for a road map to help steer your company in the right direction or simply trying to understand those concepts in more detail, if you start by reading this book, you will be starting off on your right foot.

R. Martins
Stefanini IT Solutions, Chicago, Illinois, USA

This book offers the most comprehensive view of Cloud Computing and SaaS on the market today. The author skillfully lays out a game plan for government and commercial entities alike looking to stay relevant in this burgeoning business paradigm.

K. Brown
IBM, Washington, DC, USA

Melvin Greer provides an excellent guide to the Cloud Computing IT model with a solid overview of concepts, business aspects, technical implications, benefits, challenges, and trends. Definitely a 'must read' for IT managers and enterprise architects considering adoption of this flexible, beneficial business model within their organization.

J. Magnuson
Lockheed Martin, Valley Forge, Pennsylvania, USA

This is an excerpt from Melvin Greer's book:

Software as a Service Inflection Point: Using Cloud Computing to Achieve Business Agility

Hardcover: 180 pages

Publisher: iUniverse (May 1, 2009)

Language: English

ISBN-10: 1440141959

ISBN-13: 978-1440141959

ALMOST EVERY BUSINESS REACHES a time when the fundamentals change. This time is referred to as a strategic inflection point. A strategic inflection point is a time in the life of a business when its fundamentals are about to change. That change can mean an opportunity to rise to new heights; but it may just as likely signal the beginning of the end.

Strategic inflection points can be caused by technological change, but they are more than technological change. Competitors can cause them, but they are more than just competition. Strategic inflection points are full-scale changes in the way business is conducted so that simply adopting new technology or fighting the competition, as has been done in the past, may not be sufficient. They build up force so insidiously that you may have a hard time even putting a finger on what has changed; yet you know that something has. Let's not mince words: a strategic inflection point can be deadly when unattended to. Organizations that begin a decline as a result of large-scale changes rarely recover their previous greatness.

Strategic inflection points do not always lead to disaster. When the way business is being conducted changes, it creates opportunities for players adept at operating in the new way. This can apply to newcomers or to incumbents, for whom a strategic inflection point may mean an opportunity for a new period of growth.

Over the last few years, industry has begun developing a model of information technology (IT) known as Cloud Computing, which includes Software as a Service (SaaS). This new model has reached an inflection point and will give users the choice to purchase IT as a service, as a complement to, or as a replacement of the traditional IT software/hardware infrastructure purchase. SaaS and Cloud Computing have benefits for the economy, government, innovation, energy efficiency, and competitiveness.

Adopting new technology or fighting the competition may not be enough when these critical moments arise. That's because inflection points build up force so quickly that organizations may have a hard time even putting a finger on what has changed. The way a firm responds could propel it to new heights or lead to its demise.

It is time for businesses to transform how they approach advanced software and innovative business models so they can achieve real agility. If you are a decision maker involved with the deployment of IT, then it is imperative that you understand SaaS inflection point.

THE SIGNIFICANCE OF BUSINESS AGILITY

Business agility is an organization's ability to respond to change. If the organization cannot respond well to change, it can lose competitive advantage or even cease to exist. In a world where change is more rapid and becoming less predictable, increased agility is undoubtedly critical to corporate survival. Rapid and impactful change also often presents important new opportunities. If an enterprise is less agile than its competitors, it is the competitor who will capitalize on new opportunities and grow.

There are a number of drivers forcing business agility. First, there is an increase in interconnectedness: e-mail, Web, digital supply chains, and mobile devices link us to each other in real time. Second, there are "macro" changes. These include changing market conditions, new regulations, and political situations in various parts of the world that affect business. Third, there is the growing role of information and data to improve corporate productivity. When a new medication, a new nanotechnology manufacturing technique, or an innovative marketing strategy is developed, IT is being used to increase productivity. Finally, there is profitability. Organizations are under more pressure than ever to be profitable—while, at the same time, they are faced with new challenges in achieving increased profitability.

To achieve business agility, organizations are focusing on four main areas—the components of agility: people, processes, strategy, and technology. These components are inextricably linked: if the ball is dropped on one aspect of agility, the others will suffer. For example, an organization's employees may understand how to respond to change and are motivated to do so, but if technology does not give them the information they need to observe change, they will not be able to make good decisions. If agility is built into all four components, a "virtual cycle" is created that will feed onto itself and ensure an ongoing, dynamic response to change as it occurs.

Quantifying agility involves the use of frameworks; these can be used by organizations to measure their level of agility and business value. An example of an agility framework is the Agility Quotient (AQ) tool developed by Microsoft and Gartner. The AQ tool can help organizations understand their ability to sense and respond to change as well as benchmarks their performance against industry peers. It analyzes their level of awareness, flexibility, and productivity during change and outlines tangible steps to improve. If an organization takes steps to improve agility (e.g., by upgrading its IT infrastructure), it can then use investment tools such as the Microsoft Rapid Economic Justification framework to understand the value derived from its IT investments. Many organizations have used the AQ tool to identify their level of organizational agility and to determine how to use technology to achieve an optimal state.

To survive, enterprises need a rock-solid, streamlined IT environment, but to win, they must transform their IT investment into a corporate advantage—one that drives revenue and growth and opens new markets and opportunities. Today's business climate requires a constantly evolving IT strategy that responds to new opportunities and threats on the fly. While the fundamentals of IT—reliability, availability, security, and manageability—are still crucial, rapid results are mandatory for business success. There is little room for a trade-off between reliability and agility—organizations need both.

Experts agree on the central role that agility plays. According to Gartner,[*] "Progressive companies have adopted workplace agility as a competitive imperative." Giga calls agility a "critical element to deal with

---

[*] http://my.gartner.com/portal/server.pt?objID=219&open=512&parentname=Gartner&mode=2 &parentid=0&in_hi_userid=1513914&PageID=466528&cached=false&space=Opener

continuing innovation." Agility must characterize the business itself as well as the IT infrastructure and applications on which it depends.

Research from META Group indicates that "during the operational life of complex, highly integrated systems, the largest and fastest-growing total cost-of-ownership (TCO) factor is change (i.e., adaptability). Users must continue to emphasize adaptability as their primary design goal to deliver lower TCO."

The essence of business agility is defined by John Oleson in *Pathways to Agility** as the ability to respond with ease to the unexpected. It means that the unexpected has been anticipated and the capability has been built so that the response can occur with ease.

An agile business can

- Understand market dynamics and anticipate customer needs
- Make faster decisions through better access to information
- Gain access to critical business information wherever and whenever required
- Design, introduce, or modify business services and processes
- Automatically deploy or redeploy resources based on dynamically evolving business requirements
- Maintain and improve customer service levels

Unfortunately, most organizations are more familiar with these symptoms:

- Struggling to deploy new features because of the risk of business disruption
- Supporting end-of-life or outdated proprietary systems and custom applications
- Reaching performance ceilings, yet being unable to take advantage of next-generation technologies
- Paying for underutilized assets that cannot be reused for other purposes

---

* http://www.wiley.com/WileyCDA/WileyTitle/productCd-0471191752,descCd-authorInfo.html?print=true

Today's business environment is one of rapid and continuous change; one that is marked by an increasing dependence on advanced software capability that will enable the performance of a growing number of business tasks. In this environment, the time and cost to transform information systems to respond to environmental change and the strategies developed to address that change can be a competitive advantage or disadvantage. In effect, information systems agility is becoming a larger component of enterprise agility at a time when enterprise agility is becoming more critical to enterprise success. However, many chief executive officers (CEOs) and corporate board members view existing information systems and corporate culture as primary inhibitors to strategic change. Enterprise architecture can improve information systems by creating agile advanced software methodologies, by improving development and testing environments, and by enhancing SaaS and Cloud Computing skills. However, the greatest potential gains in information systems agility will come from using enterprise architecture to develop and transmit agility-centric requirements, principles, and models for information architecture to every systems development and acquisition decision.

A well-formed SaaS and Cloud Computing inflection point strategy will be based on a strategic business vision that is derived from the enterprise's strategy and external drivers, enablers and inhibitors of change. The strategic business vision will be based not only on known and forecast process and information requirements defined by business units but also on enterprise-level "engineering requirements." In today's world of rapid and continuous change, agility is, more often than not, paramount among these engineering requirements. In an environment in which CEOs and executive teams must plan business strategy on a multiscenario basis, it is difficult for business-unit project sponsors and IT professionals to forecast process and information requirements with the accuracy necessary to define information systems process and data structures beyond the immediate future. Therefore, because forecasting requirements will not result in stable future-state information architectures, designing for agility is necessary to maintain alignment with a rapidly and continuously changing business environment. The focus on business agility is a primary driver for the rapid response and flexibility associated with the software delivery models associated with Cloud Computing and SaaS, and the main reason we have reached an inflection point with regard to their adoption.

Appendix G: FITARA and FedRAMP—Accelerating Federal Cloud Adoption

This is an excerpt from Melvin Greer's article, "FITARA and FedRAMP: Accelerating Federal Cloud Adoption," in *IEEE Cloud Computing* magazine (Vol. 2, No. 5, pp. 48–52, Sept.–Oct. 2015):

PRESIDENT OBAMA'S FISCAL YEAR (FY) 2016 budget request calls for an information technology (IT) budget of $86.4 billion for FY 2016, making the US federal government the largest buyer of IT in the world. If approved, the president's budget would invest $7.34 billion of the federal IT budget (8.5% of all IT spending) in provisioned services, such as cloud, on par with leading private-sector companies. Nearly half of the federal agencies have already moved their e-mail systems to the cloud. Federal cloud adoption is growing, led by pioneers such as the Department of Commerce, Department of Defense (DoD), General Services Administration (GSA), Health and Human Services, and NASA. These agencies are leveraging the power of Cloud Computing and have documented and distributed key lessons on how to build cloud business cases and ease organizational transitions. They're reporting that the savings are real, and the cloud can deliver on the promise of cost savings, scalability, and device agnosticism.

In its inaugural report, the Congressional Cloud Computing Caucus details the substantial progress agencies have made in adopting cloud solutions since the federal government unveiled its "Cloud First" policy in 2011. The report highlights numerous advances with regard to tracking federal security compliance across cloud service providers (CSPs) and instituting mechanisms to accelerate the adoption of Cloud Computing in the federal government. Despite this reported progress, challenges remain. The report cites a number of federal cloud adoption challenges:

- The White House FY 2016 projected cloud spend of $7.34 billion runs counter to the Office of Management and Budget's (OMB) projection of $2.1 billion.

- Only 20% of Federal workers (Feds) believe that the security offered by CSPs is sufficient.

- Some 44% of Feds say they remain "uncomfortable" or "very uncomfortable" turning IT services and applications over to cloud providers.

Two key initiatives specifically target these challenges and work to accelerate federal cloud adoption: the Federal Information Technology Acquisition Reform Act (FITARA) and the Federal Risk and Authorization Management Program (FedRAMP).

FEDERAL INFORMATION TECHNOLOGY ACQUISITION REFORM ACT

Among other things, FITARA (https://management.cio.gov), passed in December 2014, requires that all IT acquisitions be evaluated, approved, and reported by the agency chief information officer (CIO). Under FITARA, US federal CIOs must not only oversee sanctioned cloud services procured by the agency but also shadow IT, which can affect cloud adoption and increase risk. This law builds upon the Clinger–Cohen Act of 1996 (http://govinfo.library.unt.edu/npr/library/misc/itref.html) and assigns additional authority to agency CIOs. These authority enhancements include the following:

- Improved transparency and improved risk management in IT investments

- Maximized benefit of the federal strategic sourcing initiative

- Government-wide software purchasing program

- Agency-wide portfolio review

FITARA was first implemented on August 15, 2015, with agency CIOs required to submit to the OMB an IT self-assessment and FITARA implementation plan. The first step in the assessment process is the development of a common baseline, which provides a framework for agencies to implement the specific authorities that FITARA provides. This baseline is intended to provide flexibility in that agencies can adopt a plan that provides for the CIO's direct involvement or a policy approved by the CIO that contains clear rules on the procedures by which decisions are made and articulates that the CIO remains responsible and accountable for those decisions. Once the common baseline is developed, the agency performs the self-assessment, which identifies current gaps in meeting the goals associated with the common baseline, and shall articulate an implementation plan describing the changes it will make to ensure that all common baseline responsibilities are implemented by December 31, 2015. Each agency is required to perform an annual assessment to identify any obstacles or incomplete implementation of common baseline responsibilities that occurred over the preceding 12 months. The first update will be due April 30, 2016, and each April 30 on an annual basis thereafter.

Figure A7.1 shows the specific responsibilities and processes that the common baseline for IT management requires of all covered agencies. The critical assignments covered by the law include

- Budget formulation

- Budget execution

- Acquisition

- Organization and workforce

The agency CIO retains accountability for the roles and responsibilities identified in the common baseline. Because agency environments vary considerably, CIOs might find that decisions about some IT resources included in the common baseline might be more appropriately executed by other agency officials, such as a bureau CIO or even parts of program or procurement communities. This must be done in a way that allows the agency CIO to retain accountability.

The common baseline identifies specific responsibilities and processes that all covered agencies must provide at December 31, 2015.

According to a MeriTalk survey, 84% of Feds are optimistic about FITARA's ability to improve federal IT efficiency. Many point to the $12 billion in potential reduction of wasteful spending and 41% say it will reduce duplicative systems. More than 40% say it will improve the OMB IT dashboard and provide better transparency to IT projections.

Section	Common baseline for IT management			CIO assignment plan (optional)
	Budget formulation	Budget execution	Aquisition	Organization and workforce
Visibility	A1: Visibility of IT resources plans/decision to CIO A2: Visibility of IT resources plans/decision in budget materials	F1, F2: Visibility of IT expenditures reporting to CIO		
Planning	B1, B2: CIO role in pre-budget submission for programs C1, C2: CIO role in planning program management		I1: Shared acquisition and procurement responsibilities	P1, P2: IT workplace planning
Governance		H1, H2: CIO role program governance boards F2: Participate with CIO on governance boards J1: CIO role in modification, termination, or pause of IT G1: CIO defines IT processes and policies	K2: CAO is responsible for ensuring contract actions which require IT are consistent with CIO-approved plans and strategies I1, I2: Shared acquisition and procurement responsibilities	Q1: CIO reports to agency head (or to deputy/COO)
Program collaboration		E1, E2: ongoing CIO engagement with program managers		N1, N2: CIO role in ongoing bureau CIOs' evaluation O1, O2: Bureau IT leadership directory
Certifications and approvals	D1, D2: CIO reviews and approves major IT investment portion of budget request	L1, L2: CIO approval of reprogramming requests	K1: CIO review and approval of acquisition strategy and aquisition plan	M1: CIO approval of new bureau CIOs

FIGURE A7.1   Common FITARA baseline for IT management.

Acceleration of federal cloud adoption depends on improved transparency, risk management, portfolio review, and reporting. Working with agency CIOs, OMB will report quarterly to Congress on the cost savings, avoidance, and reductions in duplicative IT investments resulting from agency FITARA implementation. OMB will also provide a summary of these savings by agency on a publicly accessible website. If a CIO finds that FITARA data from individual departments isn't timely and reliable, he or she can collaborate with OMB to develop a plan that includes root cause analysis, timeline to resolve, and lessons learned. If an investment has a high risk rating for three consecutive months beginning July 1, 2015, agencies must hold a TechStat session on that investment. The session must be held within 30 days of the completion of the third month. Each of these actions focused on transparency, portfolio review, and reporting will improve visibility and communication and provide the CIO risk management framework for Cloud Computing investments.

Several key questions will affect FITARA implementation.

First, how will OMB make sure agencies successfully and completely implement these requirements? OMB will work with agencies to ensure that they are meeting the common baseline in Section A of the memorandum through existing oversight methods including PortfolioStat (https://management.cio.gov). In addition, FITARA states that agencies are required to post their plans to meet the common baseline publicly, helping to enable congressional and public oversight.

Will agency CIOs become a bottleneck and impede agencies' ability to deliver their programs? FITARA is believed to be flexible and applicable to all agencies in a way that allows them to implement the law's requirements and doesn't create unnecessary bottlenecks. Given that this was a primary concern of many CIOs, the CIO assignment plan allows CIOs to assign, in a rules-based manner, certain responsibilities to other people in their department. This keeps the accountability with the CIO but allows each agency to realistically meet the law's requirements while minimizing the chance for bottlenecks.

Why are other requirements not described in the FITARA law included? Other legislation, primarily the Clinger–Cohen Act of 1996 and the E-Government Act of 2002 (www.congress.gov/bill/107th-congress/house -bill/2458), requires the director of OMB to issue management guidance for IT and electronic government activities across the government. Moreover, the FITARA law contains both specific requirements and more general requirements that require interpretation for successful FITARA implementation.

FITARA will have a positive impact because it emphasizes the importance of CIOs having influence on three key agency success factors: budgeting, contracting, and human resources. Additionally, the law emphasizes the need to adopt industry best practices and pushes for greater adoption of Cloud Computing, enterprise services, shared services, and enterprise licensing agreements.

FEDERAL RISK AND AUTHORIZATION MANAGEMENT PROGRAM

FedRAMP (www.fedramp.gov) is a government-wide program that provides a standardized approach to security assessment, authorization, and continuous monitoring for cloud products and services. FedRAMP is the result of close collaboration with cybersecurity and cloud experts from the GSA, the National Institute of Standards and Technology (NIST), the Department of Homeland Security (DHS), DoD, OMB, and the Federal CIO Council and its working groups, as well as private industry.

The FedRAMP.gov site describes the authorization of cloud systems in a three-step process:

Security assessment. The security assessment process uses a standardized set of requirements in accordance with FISMA using a baseline set of NIST 800-53 controls to grant security authorizations.

Leveraging and authorization. Federal agencies view security authorization packages in the FedRAMP repository and leverage the security authorization packages to grant a security authorization at their own agency.

Ongoing assessment and authorization. Once an authorization is granted, ongoing assessment and authorization activities must be completed to maintain the security authorization.

By establishing a common set of security controls and an independent verification system, FedRAMP enabled agencies (https://cio.gov/wp -content/uploads/2012/09/fedrampmemo.pdf) for the first time to acquire a cloud service authorized by another federal agency without having to duplicate the entire security authorization process. With its "do once, use many times across government" security approach, GSA believes that agencies are saving at least $70 million annually by using cloud services, and the Program Management Office (PMO) expects that figure to climb. The PMO report also identifies more than 1400 "cloud implementations"—or customers—across the federal government, a 41% jump in the number of CSPs, and a 32% increase in the number of accredited third-party assessment organizations (3PAOs) from January through June 2015.

FedRAMP is accelerating federal adoption of the cloud because it codifies what is meant by federal cloud security and provides a well-defined standard that cloud consumers and cloud providers can use for assessment and evaluation.

FedRAMP progress can also be measured by these key features:

Automation of reviews for faster processing. FedRAMP is looking for an open source solution to automate quality reviews and targets having a faster new process by October 2016.

High baseline pilot through the FedRAMP Joint Authorization Board. FedRAMP has identified four vendors to pilot completion of a high authorization through the FedRAMP Joint Authorization Board.

Continuous monitoring pilot for increased scale. FedRAMP hopes to provide the same types of continuous monitoring reports for agency authorizations that are created for those of the Joint Authorization Board.

Procurement guidance for agency acquisitions. FedRAMP is targeting publication of guidance on incorporating FedRAMP into acquisitions by October 31, 2015.

Trusted Internet connection (TIC) pilot. FedRAMP is working with DHS to address comments received on the TIC Overlay, and three vendors are piloting TIC through the CIO Council.

FedRAMP guidance promotes agency reuse of authorized cloud services, and it will continue to promote the idea. FedRAMP believes that adopting cloud services already authorized for use by another agency could eliminate up to 90% of the work involved with authorization.

FedRAMP future initiatives will also have a positive impact on cloud adoption. The go-forward plan will include expanding stakeholder engagement by increasing the number of agencies implementing FedRAMP, encouraging cross-agency collaboration, and fostering understanding of FedRAMP by government and industry.

It will also move to improve program efficiencies by enhancing 3PAO assessment deliverable quality and deliverables, providing a more flexible data and workflow management framework, and incorporating industry standards where appropriate.

Finally, it will continue to adapt the FedRAMP program by evolving continuous monitoring, drafting additional baselines, and enhancing integration with cyber initiatives.

Without question, the initial concerns around moving to the cloud (security, culture, control, etc.) are being countered by real-world government successful implementation. The journey to the cloud by most government agencies starts slow, with functions such as e-mail or office productivity software. FITARA and FedRAMP help agencies become more comfortable with the cloud, which leads to implementations of more cloud-based mission-critical applications. FITARA and FedRAMP are working, and together they are providing the catalyst to accelerate federal Cloud Computing adoption.

Index

This index includes the front matter and appendices. Page numbers with f, n, t, refer to figures, footnotes, and tables, respectively.

An environmentally friendly book printed and bound in England by www.printondemand-worldwide.com